Valdez

BRITISH COLUMBIA
WASHINGTON

Lost R.

Chewuch R.

Methow

Twisp R.

River

Kettle

River

Thirteenmile Cr.

Sanpoil

River

Colville

River

River

Little Pend

Oreille R.

Pend

Oreille

River

N. Fk.

Sullivan Cr.

Harvey Cr.

N. Fk.

Entiat

Mad R.

R.

Columbia

Spokane

River

Little
Spokane
R.

SPOKANE

Wenatchee R.

WENATCHEE

Yakima
Canyon

Hanford

Reach

YAKIMA

Yakima

River

River

TRI-CITIES

WASHINGTON

Palouse

River

Snake

River

Tucannon

R.

IDAHO

WASHINGTON
OREGON

N. Fk. Wenaha R.

R.

Joseph Cr.

Grande Ronde

River

Legend:

Rivers deserving Federal, or both State and Federal designation.
Rivers deserving State designation only.

WASHINGTON'S
Wild Rivers
THE UNFINISHED WORK

WASHINGTON'S

Wild Rivers

THE UNFINISHED WORK

TIM McNULTY

♦

Photographs by

PAT O'HARA

♦

Foreword by

DANIEL J. EVANS

♦

THE MOUNTAINEERS · SEATTLE

ACKNOWLEDGMENTS

A book such as this owes its existence to many more names than appear on its title page. We were dependent on the advice and expertise of numerous individuals who gave generously of their time and would like to take this opportunity to express our gratitude.

Special thanks are due to Peggy Ferber and members of The Mountaineers' Editorial Review Committee, Wild Rivers Committee, and Conservation Division, who took a special interest in seeing this book come to be.

We would also like to thank Doug and Lorrie North, Sandie Nelson, and Tim Krause of the Northwest Rivers Council; Kevin Coyle of American Rivers; Rick Rutz of The Mountaineers; Libby Mills of the Nature Conservancy; Dennis Canty and Jim Anderson of the National Park Service; Doug Houston, Bruce Morehead, Ed Schreiner, and Greg Schroer of Olympic National Park; Art DuFault of the Columbia River Gorge National Scenic Area; Lorie Bodi of the National Oceanic and Atmospheric Administration; Steve Ralph of the Point-No-Point Treaty Council; Mark Mobbs and Steve Meadows of the Quileute Tribal Fisheries Department; Bob Hayman and Steve Fransen of the Swinomish Tribal Fisheries Department; Marsha Williams of the Cowlitz Tribe; Jim Chu, Matt Longenbaugh, Al Zander, Mark Stalmaster, Dale Potter, and Brady Green of Mt. Baker - Snoqualmie National Forest; Ernie Garcia and Dick Chavez of Okanogan National Forest; Paul Sanford, Glen Hoffman, Roger Ross, Heather Murphy, Phil Jones, Corky Broadus, Phil Glass, and Susan Carter of Wenatchee National Forest; Janet Little, Rick McClure, and David Porter of Gifford Pinchot National Forest; Steve Starlund of Washington State Parks and Recreation Commission; Steve Zubalic of the Washington State Energy Office; Jeff Cederholm of the Washington State Department of Natural Resources; Bill Wood, Chris Burns, Russ Orrell and Mark Schuler of the Washington State Department of Fisheries; Mike Ragon, Woody Myers and Ken Williams of the Washington State Department of Wildlife; Mark Schulz of Riverside State Park; Duane Bolser of Lake Wenatchee State Park; Sam Angove of Spokane County Parks Department; Oscar Graham of the Skagit County Planning Department; David Mason of Fairhaven College; Frank Ancock of the Bellingham Audubon Society; Jim Howard of Friends of the Cowlitz; Carol Volk and Gary Korb of the Olympic Rivers Council; Leon and Esther Schmidt; Dennis and Bonnie White; Morey and Margaret Haggin; Vern and Ida Bailey; Tom Jay; Bruce Brown; Krista Thie; Roger Harpel; Lee Bernheisel; Mara Green; Lynn Bouker; Roy Bergstrom; Larry Dennison; Jack Zaccardo; Kennan Harvey; Gary Gray; and Nick Gunderson.

We would also like to thank Jerry Michalec of North Cascades River Expeditions and Rod Amundson of Wildwater Tours for their support and to boatmen Rick Aramburu and Bruce McGaw. To our many friends who accompanied us on our river explorations goes our thanks. And a special debt is owed to our wives, Mary Morgan and Tina Smith-O'Hara, for their unfailing support and for the Herculean patience shown during the research and preparation of this book.

Finally, we would like to dedicate the photographs in this book to the memory of Dave Faith.

Tim McNulty and Pat O'Hara

The publisher would like to thank The Mountaineers Foundation and Northwest Wilderness & Parks Conference for their financial assistance on this project.

The Mountaineers

Published by The Mountaineers
306 Second Avenue West, Seattle, Washington 98119

Manufactured in Hong Kong by Hindy's Enterprise Co., Ltd.
Cover: Boulders, moss, and leaves, Dosewallips River.
Frontispiece: Paris Creek, flowing into the Cle Elum River.
Edited by Miriam Bulmer and Steve Whitney
Cover and book design by Elizabeth Watson

Library of Congress Cataloguing in Publication Data
McNulty, Tim.
    Washington's wild rivers : the unfinished work / by Tim McNulty : photographs by Pat O'Hara.
        p. cm.
    ISBN 0-89886-170-5. —ISBN 0-89886-241-8 (pbk.)
    1. Stream ecology—Washington (State)   2. Wild and scenic rivers—Washington (State)
    3. Stream Conservation—Washington (State)
    I. Title
QH105·W2M381990   89-13562
333.91'6216'09797--dc20   CIP

CONTENTS

Autumn pool, Yakima River drainage

FOREWORD

In my lifetime I have seen the deadening of Washington rivers, but the first taming began much earlier.

Lewis and Clark floated down the Columbia, using it as a watery freeway to the Pacific Ocean, and reported back to President Jefferson on the wonders of this untouched wilderness. Ever since, western rivers were destined to be put to work to serve a growing population. Rivers were dammed, diverted, channeled, fished, used as sewers for industrial and municipal waste, and just plain used up.

The Columbia proved tougher. Not until the 1930s was this thundering cataract stilled by a new generation of dam builders. Stretch by stretch rapids were covered. As a child, I watched transfixed as the last Indian fishermen speared salmon from Celilo Falls. Eventually that, too, was flooded, and the Columbia turned into a necklace of placid lakes. Navigation was easy, hydropower fueled our modern economy, irrigation turned deserts dollar-green, but the river as Lewis and Clark saw it was gone.

My lifelong love affair with Washington's wilderness includes our rivers, for they are the creator, lifeline, and channels of access for those who hike our ridges and climb our peaks.

I have vivid memories of a clear, white winter day steelheading on the Skagit and putting the rod aside to watch scores of stately bald eagles perched in the trees. Each respectful of the other, both using but leaving untouched the river that brought us the salmon. On quite a different warm summer day I floated the Quinault, hardly fishing at all but caught by the peace of a natural river, the flash of birds overhead, and a tiny deer drinking at the river's edge. Smelt fishing on the Cowlitz and a joyous summer outing rafting on the Yakima stay as memories to be savored as years roll by.

My favorite rivers are much more personal. They are mountain brooks, usually with no name, cascading down a mountainside chattering "stop, stop" as they cross a dry steep trail. No drink is so exotic as the first sip of teeth-numbing clear mountain water. No additives, no processing. But today we are told "be careful, giardia lurks, treat your water." What have we done to nature, which sustains us? Are we doomed to retain these experiences only as memories, never to be passed on to our children? I hope not.

We still have an opportunity to preserve stretches of our rivers that flow free and unspoiled. When in doubt, we should save the maximum number of our wild and scenic rivers. If we someday need to develop them we can make that choice, but if we fail to preserve them now, we will lose that privilege forever.

Read this book carefully. Understand the extraordinary heritage we still enjoy. Recognize that Congress is the forum and that decisions made there will profoundly affect the future of our nation's rivers.

Then join in the struggle to save this legacy for our children and generations yet to come.

Daniel J. Evans
Former Governor of Washington State

River stones and riffles, Wenatchee River

The Music of Running Water

*I knew a story had begun, perhaps long ago
near the sound of water.* —Norman MacLean

Even as the first light stirs among the trees, the sound has already come to us. It has drifted up through the alders and across the small field behind the house, slipped beneath the cedar limbs and found us. A window above the bed has been left open, as much for the river as for the smaller slipstream of air, and our day is once more coaxed to life with that oldest and most pervasive of the earth's music.

For nearly a decade the voice of the river has roused my wife and me slowly out of our separate dreams, just as its quiet murmur sent us drifting off hours before. I like to think that if there is an order and unity to the flow of our days, then the river is surely a part of that. And if a poetry graces our life together, then its voice is the undulating music of running water.

It's true that on spring mornings the bird songs tend to dominate the upper registers, and we love them for it, but even then the snowmelt current of the river provides a deep and steady undertone. And while winter rains occasionally overwhelm the river by sheer dint of force (enhanced by the acoustics of a shake roof), an equal upsurge in the river's voice is never too far behind. In the aural sphere, the river's only real rival is the November wind. Rolling in ahead of the big Pacific fronts, fall winds sweep through the valleys and scour the foothills, scattering the last of the maple leaves and pruning the limbs of firs and alders with sharp lightninglike cracks. These are the winds that wake us in the middle of the night, and we know that before dawn will come the first noisy bursts of rain.

The summer creek children waded across with their pants rolled to the knee will become a river again, with a voice utterly changed from its melodic summer pitch. Now its song will call home the salmon, pooled below in the saltwater bay. And as always I'll go down to the river to watch for them, for in the downstream flow of things, the salmon make the circle complete.

Ocean cloud to mountain, river to sea, the hydrologic cycle—though readily explained by meteorology and thermal physics—is still one of the great mysteries of the natural world. We are drawn to the sound of running water as the voiceless music of that mystery, the secret the river has brought to devout listeners since the world was new.

The first people who came to our Northwest coast, ancestors of the Salish-speaking tribes who greeted European explorers, followed the music of the river down the long canyons of the Fraser. They arrived from the ice-free corridors of the interior just as the glaciers were drawing back. A nomadic people, hunters of mammoth and bison, they had not yet learned the ways of the coastal and riverine cultures that would succeed them. But even then, something in the river must have called, bringing them to this raw coast where later hunting-gathering societies would reach the apex of their cultural development in North America.

The rivers that brought the gifts of salmon and cedar, beaver and the beautiful elk, still follow their courses down from the snow mountains to the tidelands and estuaries. Villages have been transformed into cities, and a newer people have derived great wealth from the land. The voice of the river speaks not as loudly anymore, and our ears are often turned elsewhere. But the river has not forgotten us; its music remains for all who have need of it, and in its promise lies our hope for the future.

As Sealth, chief of the Suquamish, told us more than a century ago, "If we sell you our land, you must remember, and teach your children, that the rivers are our brothers, and yours, and you must henceforth give to the rivers the kindness you would give any brother."

For Mary and me, the river has been an active voice in our life together. When we were married, we hiked in to a favorite river deep in the mountains for our wedding ceremony. Now, years later, our daughter is encountering her world within the rippling cadences of the river's voice.

For Caitlin it will be a world of herons and salmon and trees, of owl hoots through the starry darkness and deer wandering past on their ancient rounds.

Our prayer for her is that this lithe and delicate music will continue throughout her lifetime, a constant touchstone wherever she goes. And that the unhampered flow of the singing river will be there for her child to listen to, when the world has come to fully appreciate the great mystery its song has to teach us.

Part 1

The Lives of a River

The first autumn rains were late that year, but when they finally arrived on the upper Soleduck River, they made up for lost time with volume. Through the long summer and into the crisp days of fall, I had been camped with our small trail crew in a grove of tall firs just above the river. We were replacing cedar puncheon bridges along the Soleduck River trail, as well as a footbridge across the river. The days were underscored by the ever-present song of the river, sometimes distant when we were deep in timber, other times quite pronounced. Throughout the early weeks of fall the river's song dwindled to a quiet murmur. Each dawn we listened for that "whoosh" in the trees, the first gust of mountain storm that would signal the end of our season. When it finally arrived, one midnight near the end of October, the pounding on the tent woke me and kept me up into the early morning hours.

The rain continued as we finished our tasks over the next few days. Occasional breaks in the clouds revealed snow-whitened trees on the slopes just above us. The river was full-throated and boisterous now. It coursed loudly over gravel bars and boulders left high and dry for weeks. As it plunged into the mossy canyon below camp, all we could see were white waves dancing through the dark trees. In the high meadows up-valley, the elk were breaking up into small migratory bands. Black bears were taking leave of their alpine berry patches, and the marmots were shoring up their burrows. But the real drama was taking place down-valley, where the first salmon were beginning to make the final climb to their spawning grounds.

All of us knew that after packing out and loading the truck, our next stop would be the falls at Salmon Cascades.

Olympic National Park is a land of rivers. They radiate out from its mountainous core and bring the steep, broken landscape to life. Over years of living and working in the Olympics, I've come to know a good many of these rivers in their various seasons and moods. But I know of no river more arresting, none more evocative or enchanting, than the Soleduck during the fall salmon runs.

To the Quileute people who for countless generations have lived at the mouth of this great river system, fished its waters, hunted its forests, and gathered roots and herbs along its coastal prairies, the river was *Solil'tak,* "sparkling water," for its clear snowmelt source. Like other Northwest coastal tribes, the Quileutes practiced a form of the "First Salmon"

◆

Overleaf: *Lower Falls, North Fork Lewis River, Gifford Pinchot National Forest*
Inset: *Red columbine*
Opposite: *Trees and snow, Soleduck River, Olympic National Forest*
This page: *Raven*

ceremony in which the first salmon caught each year was shared among the families and its bones carefully returned to the river as a prayer. There is still something magical about the appearance of the first salmon each year, and while it is no longer synonymous with our immediate survival through the coming winter, it is tied, quite closely, to our long-range future and the overall health of our region.

From the park road, Salmon Cascades is a steep torrent where the tough basalts of the Crescent Formation shoulder the river into a narrow slot. The cascades are by no means spectacular and certainly cannot compare in grandeur to Soleduck Falls a short distance up-valley. But as we parked the truck and followed the short path to the cascades, all the power and mystery of a wild river were there flashing in the torrent before us. Out of the upwell and into the white tumult leapt one after another *Oncorhynchus kisutch*, the famed wild coho salmon. Their dark shapes rocketed from the sudsing water

like tightly wound springs, backs and tails flickering wildly as they arched into the falls. No sooner would one be swallowed up than two or three others would launch their heartful riverine flight. Occasionally a male would flash sideways, lit with a rubylike incandescence, or a large female would fetch up darkly on the rocks to be swept downstream. That any would complete their climb seemed doubtful, yet once in a great while we would see a salmon rise from the torrent to thrash stubbornly over the lip of the falls and work its way up to a quiet pool to rest.

The rain once more began to fall back over us, and the river remained high and quick. It was difficult to imagine the force of the falling water, or the strength of these creatures' all-consuming drive to return to their native birthplace to spawn and die. There is nothing remotely comparable in our own natural experience, yet this unique imperative touches something deep in the human imagination. In his essay "Salmon of the Heart," poet and

"... salmon symbolize both the human soul and the living heart of the Northwest coastal ecosystem. They are the 'silver threads' that have always stitched human culture to mountains, forests, rivers, and sea ..."

sculptor Tom Jay suggests that salmon symbolize both the human soul, and the living heart of the Northwest coastal ecosystem. They are the "silver threads" that have always stitched human culture to mountains, forests, rivers, and sea: the bright reminders of our connection with the natural world.

The salmon we watched leaping against that wall of water were "summer run" coho. Having entered the mouth of the Quillayute River in August and September, their upriver journey along the Quillayute and its major tributary, the Soleduck, had taken them nearly fifty miles to these falls. Now, with the high water, they were able to continue their passage past the hot springs resort and campground to the braided channels and clear spring-fed streams where they would spawn beneath towering cedars and firs. By completing their journey, and dying after spawning, these fish perform a unique function. They alone return valuable and necessary nutrients and trace minerals from the sea, where heavy rains and rivers have carried them, back to the ecosystems of the inland forests.

A pair of ravens called back and forth from the treetops across the river, there, like us, to witness this yearly rite. For them, and for countless other bird and mammal species in the Northwest, spawned-out salmon provide an important and readily available source of nourishment at a time when wildlife populations face their most difficult and hazardous season.

♦

Clean, free-flowing rivers, and the wild native salmon runs that depend on them, have always been associated with healthy wildlife populations. The connection between salmon, bald eagles, osprey, and bears is celebrated in Native American myths and legends, and is well documented in films, photographs, and literature. But the full extent of the interdependence between migratory salmon and inland forest wildlife communities is just beginning to be understood. Studies conducted on the upper Soleduck and other Olympic Peninsula streams have yielded some surprising results. Contrary to commonly held beliefs, the great majority of spawned salmon carcasses are not washed downstream by the river but are retained in the spawning areas, particularly in smaller streams such as those used by coho. Also, their degree of utilization and the distances they are carried by birds and mammals are much greater than had been previously imagined. Among the animals in the Soleduck Valley that will feed on these coho are black bears, raccoons, weasels, minks, bobcats, Douglas squirrels, flying squirrels, deer mice, ravens, and several smaller bird species such as jays and dippers.

The same studies also suggest that the remains of salmon dragged off into streamside forests by the larger animals contribute significantly to the growth and maintenance of the forests themselves. These studies clearly demonstrate how many of the wildlife species we often associate with wilderness areas and national parks, as well as the critical habitat that maintains them, are inextricably tied to the health of entire river systems.

Biologists refer to the lush strips of vegetation that border rivers, lakes, and streams as "riparian" areas. This vegetation provides essential food and cover to many species of wildlife throughout the year. There is also a wonderful and age-old reciprocity in the ways in which riparian forests enhance salmon habitat in the rivers. By providing shade in summer, the alders, cottonwoods, willows, and maples that border most Northwest rivers and streams maintain ideal water temperatures for salmon and trout to spawn and grow. They also support countless colonies of aphids and other invertebrates that rain down into the streams and become an important source of food for fish lurking in the cool water

below. Leaves dropped by trees in the fall provide an important additional source of nutrients as they are broken down into food for aquatic invertebrates, which in turn become food for young fry being reared in the rivers. When larger streamside trees fall across a stream, they interrupt the flow of water, creating pools and gravel beds essential for salmon and trout reproduction. Fallen trees also help retain salmon carcasses, making them available for wildlife and for the forest as well. One would be hard-pressed to draw a precise line dividing river and forest, or to separate their ecologies. The more scientists learn, the more numerous, intricate, and subtle the connections appear.

Throughout the Northwest, rivers and their associated riparian communities are the veins and lifeways of the land. In the arid, eastern part of Washington, these areas account for less than five percent of the total land base, yet they provide habitat for an estimated seventy percent of the wild-life species residing there. The "thermal cover" that riparian forests provide wildlife in eastern Washington during the temperature extremes of summer and winter is particularly important. From coastal rain forest valleys to the canyons of the Columbia Plateau, river corridors serve as key migration routes for deer and elk, connecting summer and winter ranges and providing critical fawning and calving habitat during the spring.

Wildlife species and habitat needs vary greatly with geography and climate, but the singular importance of rivers for wildlife ecology is a constant throughout the Northwest. Rivers are the unifying theme of the Northwest landscape, jade-blue ribbons that bind mountain to sea, and they enrich our own lives by sustaining the life-forms that surround us.

As the first storm brought the salmon back to the upper Soleduck, it blew in sheets across the high ridges and meadows at the river's headwaters, covering the summer range of elk and

♦

Spring maples and river, Elwha River Valley, Olympic National Park

♦

Blacktailed deer, Upper Soleduck, Olympic National Park

deer with snow. Throughout the summer I'd watched elk herds grazing among the sloping meadows and snowfields. One evening I counted over sixty elk following a talus ridge above the turquoise sheen of a mountain tarn. By the early weeks of fall the cows and calves were grouped into smaller "harems," and the bulls sounded their high-pitched challenges across the cliffs and upper basins. The snows signaled the end of rutting season, and the elk would soon be retracing their own trails down the tributary drainages and along the flat, sheltered floodplains of the river.

During severe winters, when their usual forage is buried under snow, elk and deer depend on the bare limbs of maple, alder, and willow along the river channels for food. Old growth forests of the floodplain provide thermal cover and shelter from winter storms, and lichens blown down from the forest canopy are an important supplementary food supply. Throughout the winter wide-ranging predators such as coyotes and cougars visit the flood-plains, seeking deer and elk, as well as mice, shrews, and voles.

In Washington's coastal areas, spring moves up the river valleys like a fresh green tide, and openings along river corridors are early sources of herbs, grasses, and understory shrubs. Newly leafed-out shrubs provide cover and food for young calves and fawns, and the mating and nesting activity of birds is most noticeable then. New growth, moisture, and the rich diversity of vegetation enhance the breeding and rearing habitats of raccoons, river otters, striped skunks, and long-tailed weasels. Columbia white-tailed deer and bobcats are known to rely heavily on riparian areas for breeding, as do fishers and mink. During spring, mallards, wood ducks, harlequin ducks, and mergansers add touches of brilliance to the snowmelt rivers of the high forest.

♦

Northwesterners have a keen appreciation for the value of "quality habitat" for leisure activities such as hiking, fishing, and river running. That's not terribly surprising given the richness and scale of the Northwest landscape, and it's one reason why free-flowing rivers like the Soleduck play such an important role in the recreational life of the region. From wilderness backpacking to resort vacationing recreation on the Soleduck spans a wide range of activities.

The scenic drive along the Soleduck Road is probably the most easily accessible encounter with a superb, low-elevation old growth forest the Northwest has to offer. At the road's end a developed campground and the Sol Duc Hot Springs resort serve campers and vacationers who prefer a mountain setting. An easy, one-mile walk to popular Soleduck Falls draws old and young alike. The river trail continues on to the scenic alplands of Soleduck Park and the High Divide country in the heart of the Olympics, easily the most

popular backcountry destination in Olympic National Park.

Outside the park, developed campgrounds are maintained by the U.S. Forest Service and Washington's Department of Natural Resources. Whitewater boaters are giving the river increasing attention, but it tends to be sportsmen who focus on this section of the river, and recreational use here picks up dramatically with the fall salmon runs.

Beginning with the summer coho, five distinct races of Pacific salmon enter the Soleduck River, as well as a prized winter steelhead run, making this one of the most productive fishery streams in the state. Winter sport fishing also dovetails with the hunting season for elk, attracting sportsmen and recreationists to this river on nearly a year-round basis.

The Soleduck is certainly not

◆

Mount Olympus and High Divide, Upper Soleduck, Olympic National Park

unique in this regard—the same values, natural and recreational, could be listed for dozens of rivers in Washington—but it does offer a prime example of how a free-flowing river system serves multiple needs and opportunities. Usage figures developed by the Forest Service project increasing demands for these types of recreation, yet once the Soleduck flows past the boundary of Olympic National Park into Olympic National Forest, there is no formal protection to ensure that it will remain free-flowing in the years ahead.

This same uncertainty hangs over many of Washington's remaining wild rivers. Although they largely flow across public lands, the majority of their river miles lie outside of designated parks and wilderness areas that would provide protection. As a result, the rivers are open to increased logging, mining, and hydroelectric development. Dams and so-called "small-scale" hydroelectric developments are particularly destructive. To view the kinds of destruction large dams can have on a natural river system, we need look no farther than the next river drainage east of the Soleduck—the Elwha River.

♦

Ravens are acrobats of the upper air, comfortable with the winds at great heights and capable of long, noisy flights when the mood arises. If the ravens who joined us at Salmon Cascades didn't care for the prospects, it would be, for them, a relatively short flight—less than ten miles up the Soleduck Valley and south over a low dip in the timbered ridge—to the Elwha watershed. For us the drive would be longer, but not terribly so. The north-flowing Elwha shares a common divide with the Soleduck headwaters, and the upper drainages of both rivers roughly parallel one another.

The Elwha, like the Soleduck, begins in the high mountainous interior of Olympic National Park. From the

glacier- and snowcapped peaks at its headwaters, the river's jade green flow spills in riffles and cascades through forty miles of virgin forests, rocky canyons, grassy alder bottoms, and lowland valley farms to its mouth at the Strait of Juan de Fuca. The wildlife species utilizing the Elwha Valley are comparable to those of the Soleduck, and the valley experiences a similar range of recreational uses. But fall along the upper Elwha doesn't bustle with the wildlife activity that animates the Soleduck. Eagles and ravens do not congregate along the river's banks, and the rustling of black bears, mink, otters, and raccoons does not bring the autumn twilight to life. The river ecology of the Elwha differs greatly from its neighbor to the west. Though the upper portions of both watersheds share the wilderness protection of Olympic National Park, the two rivers stand in stark contrast.

At one time the chinook runs on the Elwha River were legendary. In his book *Mountain in the Clouds*, Bruce Brown noted that in 1790 Spanish explorer Manuel Quimper remarked on the size of the Elwha salmon. More recent reports from Washington's Department of Fisheries also document salmon of exceptional size. Salmon weighing one hundred pounds were common, and an estimated eight thousand chinook climbed the Elwha River each year. Most of these chinook or "tyee" salmon successfully navigated a series of steep, narrow gorges to reach their prime spawning gravels above Long Creek. Thousands of years of these migrations produced a magnificent race of fish of a kind that no longer exists in the Pacific Northwest. Chinook, coho, pink, chum, sockeye: every species of Pacific salmon in North America at one time found favorable spawning habitat in this vast river system.

Prior to the creation of the park, in 1913 and again in 1927, two dams were constructed by private concerns

"At one time the chinook runs on the Elwha River were legendary. . . . Salmon weighing one hundred pounds were common, and an estimated eight thousand chinook climbed the Elwha River each year."

on the lower reaches of the Elwha River. Despite laws in effect, neither dam was fitted with fish ladders. The result has been that for the past seventy-five years, all but the lower five miles of the Elwha watershed has been completely blocked to the upstream migration of salmon. The value of the fishery lost to the state's economy has been estimated at over $1.7 million annually; the fish's contribution to upriver forest and wildlife communities of Olympic National Park is incalculable. Recent efforts by the Park Service to transport fish around the dams have been frustrated by salmon fry dying in the turbines on their way back downstream the following year. Studies continue, and different solutions are being sought, including removal of both dams. But in the meantime, the greatest river system on the Olympic Peninsula remains barren of its most prized and vital inhabitant.

Today, many of the cascades and gorges that gave shape to the remarkable Elwha tyee are lost beneath the impounded waters of Lake Mills. Also inundated are over one thousand acres of critical lowland riparian habitat. The gravels so necessary for the future health of the remaining downstream fishery are banked up in extensive bars at the head of the lake, and the fine sediments that would periodically enrich the lower floodplain soils are slowly sifting down through the slack waters to settle on the lake bottom.

◆

The ecological destruction brought about by dams is well documented. The natural downstream movement of oxygen and organic materials is halted, affecting the survival of fry and fish eggs. Insect larvae and other fish prey are also affected. As surface waters in reservoirs warm, their chemistry changes. The resulting stagnation and increased growth of algae drastically affect the quality of the aquatic habitat. Other problems, less devastating but equally harmful to salmon and steelhead runs, result

from dredging streambeds or confining meandering streams to straightened channels. Small-scale hydroelectric dams of the type proposed for dozens of streams throughout the state further harm fish runs by disrupting and polluting streams during construction, and later by diverting substantial amounts of water through pipelines, penstocks, and turbines.

In the United States, over fifty thousand large dams have impacted nearly every major river system outside of Alaska. Here in Washington, a land graced with more than 8,000 miles of rivers, over 1,300 miles have been destroyed by dams, diversions, channelizations, or pollution. By contrast, only 180 miles of Washington's rivers have received protection from such developments through designation as national Wild and Scenic Rivers.

Passage of the Public Utility Regulatory Policies Act of 1978, which guarantees public purchase of privately generated power at current rates, has resulted in a flood of small-scale hydroelectric applications on rivers nationwide. In the five years following the act, the number of applications to the Federal Energy Regulatory Commission (FERC) for new hydropower facilities catapulted from eighteen to over six thousand. In our national forests and on other public lands in Washington, there have been as many as a dozen applications for a single watershed.

Up until now, free-flowing rivers such as the Soleduck and Dosewallips on the Olympic Peninsula; the Nooksack, Methow, Skykomish, Wenatchee, and Pratt in the Cascades; the Klickitat and upper White Salmon in the Columbia Gorge; and the Kettle, Little Spokane, Grande Ronde, Snake, and the Hanford Reach of the Columbia in eastern Washington, have managed to survive intact, largely on their own. As demands for water, power, and other resources continue to increase, decisions will be made soon that will determine the future health of these, and many more of Washington's remaining wild rivers.

The visionary conservationist Aldo Leopold, describing what he called "The Land Ethic," wrote, "A thing is right when it tends to preserve the integrity, stability, and beauty of the biotic community. It is wrong when it tends otherwise." As Washington enters its second century of statehood, it falls upon the present generation to decide how much of this irreplaceable and necessary heritage will be left to those who follow. We would do well to remember Leopold's words, and balance our desire for economic growth with an ethic that respects the health, integrity, and beauty of the free-flowing rivers that continue to grace this wide and bountiful land.

◆

Just downstream from Salmon Cascades, the river slows in a deep, rock-walled pool before breaking up in a boulder-strewn riffle. From the rocks above I could see a number of coho circling and stirring against the cobbled bottom. Several wore pale reddish-white scars across their backs and hooked snouts, tattered masks of passage. I tried to imagine the river from their perspective, a dark rippling corridor ending in an implosion of white water. The cascade itself would be invisible. I tried to imagine fifty miles of it—the long journey leading back to the beginning, at the end of life—and my imagination faltered.

It was late. The low sky was growing dark. We had hiked out in the rain with heavy packs and we were tired. Later there would be one more trip back up the valley with mules to pack out the rest of our tools and camp gear before the snow, but now it was time to head toward town.

As I turned to go, a small coho, probably a female, launched from just shy of the foot of the falls. She hit the torrent at a break, a small hollow among the rocks that served as a crucial step in navigating the upper portion of the drop. I watched closely for the flash of silver that would signal her fall back over the lip of the cascade, but it didn't come.

The coast people believed that salmon could travel freely between worlds. Upon dying, the salmon would return to their spirit world deep in the ocean and live there in houses, like people. If the First Salmon was shown the respect and reverence due an honored guest, the salmon would return to the rivers—and the people—the following year. Not having a prayer or ceremony of my own, I bowed silently to the hidden salmon, the falls, and the rain and hurried through the darkening woods to the truck.

"A thing is right when it tends to preserve the integrity, stability, and beauty of the biotic community. It is wrong when it tends otherwise."

To Save a River

Morning sun deepened the calm green flow of the Lewis River, and a small rapid shook the surface into broken splinters of light. We had been floating the river for less than an hour, and Doug North—my companion, boatman, and guide for this trip—was totally immersed in his element. During the week Doug spends his days in the downtown offices of a Seattle law firm, but a good bit of the rest of his time is spent, if not actually floating Northwest rivers, then researching, writing about, or organizing to save them. I first met Doug a few years earlier at a gathering of conservationists in Seattle when the director of the National Park Service presented him with an award for the Northwest Rivers Council's excellent work in promoting the cause of river preservation in the Northwest. Since then we had talked about rivers quite a bit, and we'd floated one or two together. On our last trip Doug told me that the Lewis was one river that "must be experienced from the water."

As our raft drifted among the green timbered lanes and filtered light of the river corridor, I had to agree. Driving in that morning, our route wound through some heavily logged sections of the Gifford Pinchot National Forest. Fresh clearcuts alternated with young stands of even-aged second growth, and the only large continuous tracts of old growth forest we saw seemed to be confined to the river corridors. Once on the river, though, it was a different world. The roads and clearcuts of the upper slopes disappeared, and a deep forest of large mossy trees lined the banks.

Like many rivers in Washington's national forests, the upper Lewis is a sanctuary of pristine, near-wilderness habitat amidst a landscape heavily skewed toward industrial timber production. "The first thing you notice running rivers in the Northwest," Doug observed, "is how natural and undisturbed they are. It's something you can't fully appreciate while driving by on the roads above them, and it begins to change the way you think about rivers." We drifted past a smooth rock shelf still in shadow but lit with clusters of bright yellow coast monkey flowers and slender arnicas. The river moved slowly through the tall forest, occasionally dancing up into choppy white rapids or pausing briefly in deep translucent pools.

Doug is an excellent boatman, and with his wife, photographer Lorrie North, has authored two whitewater guidebooks to Washington's rivers. This particular float was less a whitewater adventure than a tour down one of the state's most scenic rivers, and the slow pace

◆

Opposite: *Middle Falls, Lewis River, Gifford Pinchot National Forest*
This page: *Spotted owl*

[the battle over Hetch Hetchy Valley] ". . . was the first time in our history that the ethic of utilization of undeveloped country for the cause of civilization and progress was seriously challenged."

gave us time to talk. I was curious about Doug's involvement with river preservation in the Northwest, as well as the history of river conservation nationally.

"I'll have to take those questions one at a time," Doug laughed. "My own history with river protection only goes back about five years. I first began canoeing and river rafting in 1981. It was a wonderful time of discovery for me; many of Washington's wild rivers were virtually unknown. By 1983 I was working on my first whitewater guidebook. It was then I found that there were active proposals to dam some of the very rivers I was writing about. The deeper I dug, the more dam proposals surfaced. Once the shock wore off, I began to organize other river boaters to write letters and oppose these dams, and the Northwest Rivers Council eventually grew out of that.

"On the national level though, river conservation has a long and illustrious history. It first became an issue in the early 1900s with the battle over Hetch Hetchy Valley in Yosemite National Park."

I remembered the account from Roderick Nash's excellent study *Wilderness and the American Mind*. Nash called Hetch Hetchy "the first great conservation controversy in American history." It seems appropriate that it should have centered around one of the first great conservation leaders in our history, John Muir. Muir had worked diligently to secure the preservation of Yosemite, and he saw it declared a national park in 1890. North of Yosemite Valley in the park, the Tuolumne River paused in its descent from the high Sierra to meander through the pristine meadows and groves of Hetch Hetchy Valley.

Muir referred to the valley as the Hetch Hetchy Yosemite, "a wonderfully exact counterpart of the Merced Yosemite, not only in its sublime rocks and waterfalls, but in the gardens, groves and meadows of its flowery park-like floor." But in 1901 the city of

San Francisco filed for rights to construct a dam for hydroelectricity and a municipal water supply that would completely flood Hetch Hetchy Valley. The battle that ensued quickly spread from California to the United States Congress. It spilled into the national press and Hetch Hetchy soon became a national issue. At stake were not only a river and its valley, preservationists maintained, but the integrity of the fledgling national park system itself.

In 1908 the permit for construction was issued, and Muir, then seventy years old, redoubled his efforts. As always, Muir was both eloquent and hard-hitting in his plea.

These temple destroyers, devotees of raging commercialism, seem to have a perfect contempt for Nature, and instead of lifting their eyes to the God of the mountains, lift them to the Almighty Dollar.

Dam Hetch Hetchy! As well dam for water tanks the people's cathedrals and churches, for no holier temple has ever been consecrated by the heart of man.

Though memorable, Muir's words proved no match for San Francisco's well-orchestrated lobbying effort in Washington, D.C., and in 1913 President Woodrow Wilson signed the bill authorizing the dam. It was a major defeat for Muir and his followers, and Muir died a year later. Yet as Nash has pointed out, it was the first time in our history that the ethic of utilization of undeveloped country for the cause of "civilization and progress" was seriously challenged. This challenge, which was based on recreational, aesthetic, and inspirational values, opened a new epoch in Americans' attitudes about the land.

"The thing to keep in mind about Hetch Hetchy and the other early river battles," Doug continued, "is that the issue wasn't necessarily the river itself, but the landscape that was threatened with flooding. It would be another half century before Americans were moved

to defend the intrinsic values of rivers themselves. And it would take the destruction of many more of our finest rivers to bring this about."

We had passed under a bridge and entered a narrow gorge. The mossy walls were deep in shadow, and delicate fronds of maidenhair fern hung from the rock. The river was deep and calm, and the song of a dipper echoed among the walls. A set of bouldery rapids loomed ahead at a curve in the river, and just beyond them a smaller rapid curled out of a deep shadowed pool into the sunlight. Not far ahead was Curly Creek Falls, a place Doug

◆

Curly Creek Falls, Lewis River, Gifford Pinchot National Forest

"As we drew near, a falling column of water emerged from behind a steep, mossy cliff. The falls plunged from a notch some seventy feet above us, and cascaded behind a stunning double rock archway before crashing into a pool along the river."

had described in *Washington Whitewater 2* as one of the most beautiful sights on any Washington river.

From just upstream we could hear the rush of the falls and see mist billowing into the sunlight. As we drew near, a falling column of water emerged from behind a steep, mossy cliff. The falls plunged from a notch some seventy feet above us, and cascaded behind a stunning double rock archway before crashing into a pool along the river. We pulled up below the falls and let the wind and spray wash over us, then rowed back across the river for lunch in the warm sunlight. As we sat among mossy boulders crowded with bluebells, our talk once more turned to rivers.

"It's funny," Doug began. "For decades after Hetch Hetchy, the controversies over dam construction centered not over whether certain dams *should* be built, but *who* should build them. In Washington, beginning with the Bonneville Dam in 1938 and continuing throughout the entire damming of the Columbia River, the issue was not fish or treaty rights or recreation or aesthetics, but public versus private power development. It wasn't until the 1950s that opposition to the Mossy Rock Dam on the Cowlitz centered on destruction of the salmon runs."

The Columbia is the largest and most complex river system entering the Pacific, yet of its 1,243-mile length, only fifty miles remain free-flowing, nearly all of this within the Hanford Reach. The Northwest Power Planning Council estimates that 4,600 stream miles of the Columbia River basin's salmon and steelhead spawning and rearing habitat have been destroyed. Of the ten to sixteen million salmon and steelhead that historically plied the Columbia's waters, only 2.5 million remain today. Some 75 percent of this loss has been directly related to dam construction, and cumulative losses to Northwest fisheries may number in the billions of dollars. While

producing the nation's cheapest electricity, we in the Northwest have traded off another source of wealth. And though fishermen and Indian tribes objected, their voices were lost in the New Deal clamor for federally funded jobs and publicly produced power.

Passage of the 1936 Flood Control Act triggered a national agenda of dam construction, and created a small empire ruled by the Army Corps of Engineers. Its authority, along with that of the Federal Bureau of Reclamation, would rule America's waterways unchallenged for years to come.

"The next major environmental challenge to a dam didn't come until 1943," Doug continued, "when the Bureau of Reclamation proposed the infamous Echo Park Dam in Colorado."

This 525-foot dam would have flooded Echo Park and the canyons of the Green and Yampa rivers in Dinosaur National Monument. Debate over the project raged on for years, and national environmental groups banded together to make Echo Park the environmental cause of the 1950s. Pivotal in the campaign to stop the dam was the Sierra Club, led by its young executive director, David Brower. Brower, an imaginative and dedicated spokesman for the environment, brought a new level of passion and intensity to the environmental dialogue: "When a living heritage is being put to death—perpetual, eternal, permanent death—there is no fairness in giving the attacker and savior equal time." Like John Muir a half century earlier, Brower became a champion of park and wilderness protection; and just as with the Hetch Hetchy project, conservationists saw the Echo Park Dam as a dangerous precedent that threatened to reopen previously proposed projects in other national parks throughout the West.

At congressional hearings held in 1954, Brower showed photographs of Hetch Hetchy Valley before and after

♦

Rafting the Lewis River, Gifford Pinchot National Forest

the dam, along with stunning photographs of Echo Park. "If we heed the lesson learned from the tragedy of the misplaced dam in Hetch Hetchy," he told a Senate subcommittee, "we can prevent a far more disastrous stumble in Dinosaur National Monument." The conservation movement had learned some lessons since their defeat at Hetch Hetchy, and their campaign for Dinosaur employed mass mailings, national press coverage, films, and the prose of such eloquent writers as Bernard DeVoto and Wallace Stegner. A large-format book, *This is Dinosaur: Echo Park Country and its Magic Rivers,* was published and distributed to every member of Congress, and letters were written by the thousands. The end result was a hard-won victory, in 1955, when Congress withdrew the Echo Park Dam from the Upper Colorado River Storage Project. In so doing, however, Congress approved the other dams in the project, thus sealing the fate of another spectacular Southwest canyon, Glen Canyon on the Colorado.

David Brower later referred to Glen Canyon as the greatest loss of wilderness in his lifetime. Martin Litton, a Sierra Club activist at the time, summed it up like this: "If we hadn't believed in ourselves enough, we never would have stopped the Dinosaur thing. If we had believed in ourselves enough, we would have stopped Glen Canyon Dam on the Colorado River." Fueled by such sentiment, environmental groups were able to level all their guns at a later Bureau of Reclamation plan to build two dams in the Grand Canyon.

The proposal to construct dams in Grand Canyon National Park became the largest single river campaign yet, and it prompted Brower to take out the now-famous full-page advertisements in the *New York Times* and the *San Francisco Chronicle* that asked the rhetorical question, "Should we flood the Sistine Chapel so tourists can get nearer the ceiling?" The Grand Canyon campaign sparked the imagination of the American people, and it was a resounding success. In 1967, when Secretary of the Interior Stewart Udall finally dropped his support for the

◆

Wood violets, Lewis River, Gifford Pinchot National Forest

dams, he credited public opinion and a raft trip down the Grand Canyon with changing his mind.

"An interesting aspect of the Dinosaur and Grand Canyon campaigns," Doug mentioned, "was that for the first time, conservationists utilized raft trips down the river canyons as a way of building support for saving rivers." We had finished our lunch and Doug was pushing the raft back into the river. He pulled at the oars to get us out into the current, then relaxed. After a short pause he looked up. "River awareness has been slow to develop in this country," he said. "It hasn't achieved the popularity of wilderness preservation, yet rivers are often more accessible, less demanding to visit, and biologically just as important as larger wilderness areas. It's puzzling."

In 1984, Doug founded Friends of Whitewater, an association of whitewater boaters and guides, "to protect and enhance the natural values of

Northwest rivers through advocacy, public education, and coordination of citizen effort." As the group's membership began to swell with fishermen, hikers, campers, and other conservation-minded river users, it changed its name to the Northwest Rivers Council. After serving four years as president, Doug recently stepped down to head the organization's conservation committee. Along with the National Park Service award, the Northwest Rivers Council was also distinguished by the national organization American Rivers as "an outstanding river advocacy group." With all of Doug's efforts on behalf of rivers, his float trips have become fewer and farther between. I asked if he found this a bit frustrating? "No," he laughed. "It just makes me appreciate each river more when I do get to boat them."

Below Curly Creek Falls we entered a wide reach of flat water flowing over a clear gravel bottom. An osprey dropped from a limb and flapped slowly downstream; sunlight reflected against the trees. Ahead of us the river ran to a cliff wall fringed with wildflowers, then took a sharp bend to the right. As a yearling doe watched us from an alder thicket on a small gravel island, Doug picked up his thread of thought and continued.

"Ultimately, it took a pair of wildlife biologists, the Craighead brothers, to envision a system of nationally protected rivers, much like our system of nationally protected wilderness areas." I knew of John and Frank Craighead's pioneering work on grizzly bears in the northern Rockies—Frank Craighead's book *Track of the Grizzly* has become the standard in its field—but I didn't know the brothers were also river enthusiasts. "Up through the fifties, river protection in America had been a series of rear-guard actions, reacting to various dam proposals," Doug continued. "From their experiences on the upper Snake River, and the Middle Fork Salmon in Idaho, the Craigheads realized that the wild rivers of the West wouldn't remain wild and free-flowing for long without some means of protecting them."

In a 1957 magazine article, John Craighead was already emphasizing the importance of free-flowing rivers to upstream wilderness areas: "Rivers and their watersheds are inseparable, and to maintain wild areas we must preserve the rivers that drain them." Having worked on the National Wilderness Act, Craighead proposed a system of federally protected rivers in 1959. The idea caught on immediately with conservationists and by the early sixties various government agencies and commissions were considering different options for river protection. Individual river bills were proposed and several rivers were studied.

Finally, in 1968, after much hard work and a few false starts, the National Wild and Scenic Rivers Act was signed into law. The act designated portions of eight rivers and initiated studies for twenty-seven others. The only Northwest river designated under the act was the Rogue in southern Oregon. Here in Washington, the Skagit was listed as a study river under the act, and it was added to the system in 1978. The Klickitat and White Salmon rivers were included in 1986. In 1977 Washington state passed its own State Scenic Rivers Act, and the Skykomish became the first in the state's Scenic Rivers program.

Doug had threaded our raft through a series of channels that wound past islands in the river. Now that the river had opened up some, he was able to sit back and gather his thoughts. "The National Wild and Scenic Rivers Act was a landmark piece of legislation. For the first time conservationists had a national vehicle for preserving rivers without having to fight dams on a piecemeal basis in Congress. The act prohibits dams and other federal projects, regulates development along adjacent shorelines to a degree, and provides for public access. Most of all it preserves designated rivers in their current state, and gives hope to groups like ours that are trying to save other beautiful stretches of river—like this one."

As we neared the end of our float, and the Muddy River flowed into the Lewis from the north, the landscape changed dramatically. A large clearcut down to the river opened to a view of stripped-off ridges to the north. The shattered profile of Mount St. Helens rose over the foothills, somber and ghostlike, and the flow of the river slowed as it approached the stilled waters of Swift Reservoir.

Eagle Cliff Drop was our last rapid. As we approached it, Doug explained some of the cutting. "A fourth dam on the Lewis was proposed for this spot. The Eagle Cliff Dam, if built, would have backed water over the entire reach we just floated. The project isn't dead; they almost never are. It's just been placed on hold until the economics look more favorable. In the meantime, we're hoping to get this part of the river included in the Wild and Scenic system."

Doug swung the raft wide to the left, and we ran the drop down a choppy stairstepped bank of waves and into the calm water below. As we pulled over to our takeout, two young boys were wading in sunny pools among boulders at the river's edge.

"You guys come from way up the river?" they asked.

"Sure did."

"What's it like up there?"

After thinking for a moment, I answered, "It's like no place I've ever been before," and watched as their gazes followed up the shimmering reach to that roving corridor hidden among the great trees.

"Rivers and their watersheds are inseparable, and to maintain wild areas we must preserve the rivers that drain them."

The Skagit Wild & Scenic River System

Libby Mills looked up from her spotting scope and then scanned the gravel bar on the river below us. "Four juveniles and an adult." As I looked through the scope I could see them, feeding on a spawned salmon, pacing in that deliberate yet slightly awkward gait, taking turns as they fed. But another adult had just flown in and landed. Was it the one we had counted earlier, perched in a tree now hidden from sight? "It may be," Libby answered. "I won't add him to the count, but let's keep an eye on him."

Keeping an eye on them was easier said than done. It seemed that bald eagles were literally dropping from the trees along the Skagit River that early December morning, gliding slow and heavily down to the cobble banks of the river or landing in limbs of the cottonwoods and alders that crowded the river's shorelines. As steward for the Nature Conservancy's Skagit River Bald Eagle Natural Area, it was part of Libby's job to take a weekly census along the river between Rockport and Marblemount throughout the wintering season when bald eagles flocked to the Skagit. This was the first stop of her first census of the year, and already the eagles were making things difficult.

A lone eagle left its perch and flapped slowly upriver as two more suddenly appeared on the gravel bar below us. Libby carefully recorded the data: age, perching site, distance from the river, activity. . . . She looked up from her chart with a smile. "If you think this is confusing, you should have been here in 1982, the year I started. It was a record year for the chum run and eagles were everywhere. I didn't know the river well then, and I went crazy trying to record all the data. There were about fifty eagles at each corner of the river. My highest count in one spot was 104!"

From our vantage point on a trail that skirted the edge of a bluff above the river, we had an excellent perspective. It was easy to pick out the white heads and tail feathers of the adults perched against the dark background of bare winter limbs. Across the river, the forest rolled back in thick ranks of evergreens to the snowy upper slopes of a ridge whose crest was hidden in a wintery gray ceiling of cloud. The river curved through a wide bottomland and fingers of mist rolled up the creek gorges.

The Skagit supports one of the largest wintering bald eagle populations in the lower forty-eight states. Depending on the size of the chum salmon run each year, and the severity

◆

Opposite: *Autumn leaves, Skagit River*
This page: *Bald eagle*

"Bald eagles seem to habitually use the same roost sites, following the creek drainages up from the river, and returning downstream at first light."

of the winter, as many as six hundred northern bald eagles may winter along the Skagit and its tributaries. Most come from British Columbia and southeast Alaska, where earlier salmon runs have tapered off. Radio-collared eagles from as far north as Haines, Alaska, and as far east as Glacier National Park in Montana have been recorded on the Skagit. Their annual winter journey is a migratory pattern that may well date back thousands of years, and it points to a critical function of our temperate coastal rivers, and the wild salmon runs they harbor.

As we walked back through the forest toward the highway, I asked Libby about the seasonal pattern of eagle use on the Skagit. "Most years, the eagles begin arriving in mid-November, with the last of the coho runs. Their numbers increase dramatically as the winter chum run builds throughout December, reaching a peak in mid-January. But what's more fascinating to me are the eagles' daily patterns once they're here."

Along the highway, Libby pointed out patches of old growth forest up the side canyons and draws of the valley

◆

Opposite: *Bald eagles and cottonwood, Skagit River near Rockport*

This page: *Libby Mills at work, Skagit River, Rockport State Park*

slopes. These are the kinds of sites the eagles select for their communal night roosts. One known roost was in a ragged stand of old trees just above where we stopped. Biologists believe these multilayered stands offer a degree of thermal cover during cold winter nights. Bald eagles seem to habitually use the same roost sites, following the creek drainages up from the river, and returning downstream at first light. Libby noted that the early hours of feeding are most important for eagles, and by midmorning feeding activity is at its height. Adults sometimes squabble over the large chum carcasses, and it's common to see a feeding eagle surrounded by a subcommittee of pesky crows. After feeding they repair to nearby perch trees, returning to the river to feed as the need arises.

"Unfortunately, early morning is also the time steelhead fishermen like to drift the river, and eagles are very sensitive to human presence—unlike the more cheeky crows and gulls, who just go right on feeding." She reminded me that many of these birds probably spend most of their lives in some fairly remote regions.

Late in the day, many of the Skagit eagles take part in an activity that remains something of a puzzle to biologists. They gather in different "staging areas" along the river—a large old maple tree or a cluster of alders—before returning to their night roosts in the forest. Those scientists who are naturally prone to speculation let their imaginations fly on this question while their more rigid-thinking colleagues cite the lack of data and defer judgment. One biologist I spoke with suggested, quite sensibly, that staging eagles may simply be exchanging information on the condition of the runs. It's known that eagles fly from the staging areas to their night roosts in groups, so it may be that they gather to ensure that the young and newly arrived to the river can find their way to the selected roosts. Given the fact that an eagle may visit a number of river drainages over a winter, this also makes

"The Skagit . . . contains some of the finest spawning and rearing habitat in the state. It is Washington's only large river system that still maintains viable and healthy stocks of native fish species."

good sense.

I asked Libby how she first became interested in eagles. "Well, I remember the day I first saw them. It was seventeen years ago in the San Juan Islands and I was twenty." In the years that followed, Libby finished her undergraduate work in biology and went to work for the National Park Service: the Olympics, Mount Rainier, and the place most Park Service biologists dream of working, Alaska. "At Katmai, where I worked for several seasons, I was continually surrounded by eagles. And salmon, of course." It was also in Alaska that she first began to work with another species that feasts on salmon—bears. But she gave up the Alaska wilds to return to her native Washington, and the wintering eagles of the Skagit.

"What attracted me to this job was the opportunity to combine wildlife and habitat work with talking to kids in grade schools. That, and being able to talk with people along the river, alerting them to the eagles' needs. For me, it's the perfect combination." The rest of her time seems well taken up with equally varied pursuits. Her work as a graphic artist vies for time with photography, volunteer conservation work, folk dancing, sea kayaking. . . . "Actually, three months a year with the eagle preserve is just about right."

We had stopped at a place where the river cut close to the highway in a broad sweep of gravel and riffling gray-green water. Below us, eight or nine female salmon were sitting over their redds in a shallow side channel, tails moving lightly with the current, while several spent salmon lay cast up on the gravel around them.

In years when chum runs are down, eagles wintering on the Skagit will feed on coho and sockeye, other species of salmon native to the river. The Skagit is the largest river system in western Washington, and contains some of the finest spawning and rearing habitat in the state. It is Washington's only large

river system that still maintains viable and healthy stocks of native fish species. With waves of spawning activity occurring nearly year-round, the Skagit system supports a vigorous sport, commercial, and tribal fishery, all of which are important components of the local economy. Distinct runs of spring and summer chinook, pink, coho, and sockeye salmon share the river with winter steelhead and, of course, the winter chums so important to the eagles.

Russ Orrell is the North Puget Sound regional biologist for Washington's Department of Fisheries, and for the past twenty-five years he's kept a close eye on the Skagit and its salmon populations. "The Skagit is as good as any river for individual runs," he told me, "but when you consider all the species of native runs in the state, the Skagit has to be considered the best river for wild fish." Steve Fransen, habitat biologist for the Swinomish tribe, agrees. He attributes the high quality of fish habitat in the Skagit to a combination of factors that he summarizes as "a mixture of geography and politics." The fact that so much of the steep, mountainous upper watershed of the river system is protected from logging and development by North Cascades National Park and the wilderness areas of the Mount Baker–Snoqualmie National Forest ensures that the quality of the aquatic habitat remains high. This benefits not only the fish, but fishermen and a large community of wildlife in addition to bald eagles. In the Cascades, this community includes wolverines at the higher elevations, and quite possibly grizzly bears.

◆

When Congress passed the Wild and Scenic Rivers Act in 1968, it identified the Skagit as one of the rivers to be studied for potential inclusion in the Wild and Scenic system. Due to its wealth of wild fish runs, and because bald eagles had been classified as "threatened" or "endangered" in all states except Alaska, wildlife managers

and conservationists had focused special attention on the Skagit as a critical winter habitat. When the study was completed in 1977, it identified these values as worthy of preservation, and a year later Congress designated the Skagit as part of the National Wild and Scenic Rivers System.

The Skagit was Washington's first Wild and Scenic River, and remains its largest. Some 158 miles of the Skagit and its Sauk, Suiattle, and Cascade river tributaries comprise the system. The Skagit River is protected from just east of the town of Sedro Woolley, upstream to the Ross Lake National Recreation Area. The Sauk, Suiattle, and Cascade rivers are protected from their confluences with the Skagit, upstream to the Glacier Peak Wilderness Area. Included in the Wild and Scenic corridor are the rivers, their channels, sloughs, and banks, much of their floodplains, and some of the timbered breaks above, including the prime perching sites for eagles.

In the study that lead to its 1978 designation, the Skagit was identified as being "outstandingly remarkable" in its fishery, wildlife, and scenic resources. As a result, the Forest Service, which is the agency charged with management of the Skagit system, was directed by legislation to "preserve and enhance" these three qualities.

◆

The Wild and Scenic Rivers Act identifies three levels of protection for designated rivers. These reflect a river's degree of naturalness, and the kinds of uses a river is providing at the time of designation. A "Wild River" is free-flowing, unpolluted, and generally accessible only by trail. Its shorelines are primitive and show no signs of development.

A "Scenic River" is also free-flowing but may be a bit more developed. A Scenic River can have some road access and limited residential development along its shoreline. Farming and timber cutting are also permitted as long as they do not detract from the river's natural character. In the Skagit system, the Sauk, Suiattle, and Cascade are all Scenic Rivers.

A "Recreational River" is more developed and readily accessible by road. This classification allows for a full range of agricultural and forestry uses and may contain residential and commercial properties. The Skagit River itself has been designated a Recreational River. These classifications do not

◆

Eagles and mergansers, Nature Conservancy Skagit River Bald Eagle Natural Area

"The main thrust of a Wild and Scenic designation is to maintain and protect a river in its current natural state."

mean that "scenic" or "recreational" uses are the main value of these rivers. They are simply categories to ensure that any outstanding river might qualify for protection regardless of its degree of shoreline development.

The main thrust of a Wild and Scenic designation is to maintain and protect a river in its current natural state. No dams or destructive water projects are allowed, but farms, homes, and cabins along the river can continue to be used just as they were before. On the whole the act seeks to strike a balance between rivers already allocated to development and those that will be protected forever. On the Skagit, this idea of balancing uses is particularly appropriate since the river's uppermost reach, and its Baker River tributary to the north, were long ago dammed for hydroelectric production. With the middle Skagit and its major tributaries now Wild and Scenic, the river's outstanding natural qualities will be preserved, and human uses of all kinds, from whitewater rafting to dairy farming, will continue amid the scenic beauty of one of the Northwest's most vital rivers.

♦

As Wild and Scenic River manager for the Mount Baker District of the National Forest, it's Jim Chu's job to see that the fish, wildlife, and scenic values of the Skagit Recreational River are maintained. This portion of the system, which includes all of the main stem of the Skagit, lies on private lands outside of the National Forest. Salmon, eagles, and other wildlife obviously pay little heed to administrative boundaries, but it is a concern for managers. The Forest Service has jurisdiction over the surface waters of the river, but federal laws do not apply to private lands along the shoreline. As Jim sees it, the Forest Service is in "a monitoring mode" on this part of the Wild and Scenic corridor. "Our emphasis here is to ensure that state and county ordinances such as shoreline,

zoning, and floodplain restrictions are enforced. So I spend a lot of time working with local governments to see if, in fact, existing regulations *are* working, and if any of them need to be changed."

In this capacity the Forest Service has provided comments and suggested modifications on proposed projects both within and outside the Wild and Scenic corridor that might affect river values. These have included hydroelectric developments, powerline projects, and logging plans. Jim also works closely with fishing guides and rafting outfitters—two user groups whose numbers have soared in recent years—to make sure their activities on the river cause a minimum of disturbance to feeding winter eagles. Other Forest Service activities in the corridor include a series of informational displays and a seasonal interpreter whose educational efforts will influence both the use and appreciation of the Skagit system.

It's an unusual role for the Forest Service—to be custodian of lands other than its own—but one many conservationists feel represents a positive direction for the agency to take. Dale Potter, a planner for Mount Baker–Snoqualmie National Forest, explains the Forest Service's role like this: "We have the authority to purchase lands from willing sellers along the Wild and Scenic River corridor, but based on our experience with other rivers, we don't see that as a possibility on the Skagit. We'd rather direct our efforts toward working with the county and state to enforce existing regulations and laws."

Since the Skagit Wild and Scenic River system is more than 50 percent in public ownership (as are nearly all proposed Wild and Scenic rivers in the state), the Wild and Scenic Rivers Act expressly forbids the federal government from acquiring any private lands within the corridor by condemnation. Easements for access or scenic protection may be purchased, but these too have proven unnecessary on the Skagit. In fact, life along the Skagit seems to have changed very little since the river was declared Wild and Scenic.

◆

It was late in the day when I walked with Libby down a grassy tractor road that bordered a wide spreading pasture and farm set among timbered foothills. The mountains were still hidden in winter clouds, and a sizable creek cut down from the hills and joined the river amid cottonwoods on the far side of the pasture. The river here meandered in a broad series of sloughs, channels, and alder-covered islands. These slow-moving streams are excellent spawning and rearing habitat for chum salmon, and their seclusion and distance from roads make them an ideal haunt for eagles. This was our last stop for the day, and I thought, when Libby described it as a spot where she sometimes doubles her count, that she was exaggerating. But as we entered the grassy bottomland by the river, grown up in alder and young fir, I stopped short.

Several eagles rose noisily from a gravel bar, and groups of eagles perched in clusters among the trees along either side of the channel. All the while Libby was taking her count, eagles were gliding down to the riverbanks and passing back and forth above the channels through the groves of trees. A group of eight adults sat in a large maple that leaned out over a channel, and nearly every step I took brought new birds into sight. I found myself repeating the description I'd heard so often from fishermen friends, of the eagles in Southeast Alaska being "like crows." And they were! As dense and as busy.

Somewhere nearby, among the limbs of a great mossy maple or cottonwood, a group of eagles would soon gather, then lift off in a group and follow the creek corridor beyond the pastures and farm buildings, beyond the

paved road and the rising hills grown up with stands of second growth, into the steeper country of the national forest. There, four miles upstream, one of a handful of known night roosts remains in a dense stand of old growth fir. In an hour or two the first eagles would drift down into the open canopy to the stout limbs of an old fir, ruffle their feathers, and hunker down for another night.

This site, like most of the known roost sites, lies outside the protected river corridor, but it's nonetheless essential to the birds' welfare. For reasons such as this, many conservationists feel that the Wild and Scenic system on the Skagit needs to be expanded. They cite important yet unprotected tributary streams like Illabut and Big Beaver creeks, and other drainages presently threatened with hydroelectric development, like Thunder and Diobsud creeks and the remaining free-flowing portion of the Skagit upstream to Newhalem.

I caught up with Libby in a grove of alders where she was completing her count. We had come to this part of the river with a running count of fifty-seven eagles for the nine-mile reach of river between Rockport and Marblemount. As Libby finished her tally she announced the final count for the reach. "One hundred and eight! Not too bad for the beginning of the season." I guessed that was probably more eagles than I'd seen in the last three years combined, and I had to admit it made me a little dizzy.

Maybe it was the 4:00 A.M. rise for the ferry; maybe my mind was ceasing to work. But I imagined the eagles counting the counters. The familiar tall blonde woman with tweed cap and clipboard. And this other fellow trailing behind scribbling into a small yellow notebook. "Two! Not bad for the beginning of the biologist season." And I smiled to myself as we closed the pasture gate.

"Somewhere nearby, among the limbs of a great mossy maple or cottonwood, a group of eagles would soon gather, then lift off . . . and follow the creek corridor . . . into the steeper country of the national forest."

Part 2

Nooksack

Evening light had softened the texture of the hanging glaciers and icefalls, and shadows began to climb the polished walls of the cirque. Traces of cloud gathered about the high summits of the headwater peaks, and the air grew chill. Across the meltwater torrent, a band of mountain hemlocks caught the last light falling up-valley, and delicate wisps of lichen glowed beneath their boughs. A warbler trilled from a small tree behind us, while all around the low roar of falling water echoed off sheer mountain walls.

A friend and I were camped on a river terrace above the wide cobbled floor of Nooksack Cirque in the heart of the North Cascades. We had hiked in that afternoon with hopes of climbing Cloudcap Peak early the next morning. I'd been turned back by a storm the year before, and we had hoped, as we started out from Bellingham that morning, that the window of good weather would hold. But the clouds forming around the peaks and the dark ominous wall moving in from down-valley suggested otherwise. We knew the next day would bring only a wet slog out in the rain. Our goal abandoned, we settled back with a second pot of tea and took in one of the most dramatic mountain landscapes in the Northwest.

Nooksack Cirque forms the headwaters of the North Fork of the Nooksack River. Here, amid granite walls that rise three thousand to four thousand feet into some of the most rugged and splendid peaks in the range, the Nocksack finds its source. Threadlike waterfalls ribbon the cliff walls on three sides, draining the high glaciers and snowfields. Tumultuous streams plunge through narrow cuts and gullies, thunder beneath snow tunnels, and spill over smooth slabs and ledges before losing themselves in the cobbles and boulders of the cirque floor.

The cirque is a landscape of great power and presence, dominated by the classic forms of Mount Shuksan and Nooksack Tower, and bounded by the broken sawteeth of Jagged Ridge and Cloudcap Peak, and the glacier-smoothed skirts of Icy Peak and Ruth Mountain. There are few sites anywhere in the North Cascades more starkly beautiful, yet its beauty reveals the primal forces of uplift, ice, and flowing water that gave shape to this landscape and to the vast wilderness that surrounds it. Here, as clearly as anywhere, one can witness first-hand the overwhelming role glaciers have played in carving these moun-

◆

Overleaf: *Cloudcap Peak and East Nooksack Glacier, upper Nooksack River, North Cascades National Park*
Inset: *Ponderosa pine*
Opposite: *Nooksack Falls in winter, Mount Baker-Snoqualmie National Forest*
This page: *Avalanche lily*

tain landscapes, and in shaping the present-day courses of the streams and rivers that drain them.

♦

During the three to four million years of the Pleistocene, as the young Cascade Range continued to rise, the mountains trapped storm fronts moving in from the Pacific and accumulated vast amounts of snow. As the snow compacted, year after year, it solidified into ice and began to flow downhill as glaciers, quarrying rock and rubble from the mountain slopes. This material, combined with the great weight of the ice, over millennia, allowed the glaciers to carve out the magnificent cirques, deep U-shaped valleys, steep-sided towers, and sharp, broken ridges that so typify the North Cascades. At Nooksack Cirque, glacial scouring from three sides carved—out of the tough granite core of the mountains—a magnificent amphitheater. In all aspects, it is a landscape newly emerged from the ice.

Here, over the boulder-strewn rubble that covers the cirque floor, the ice-melt streams gather, and the Nooksack River begins its westering course to Puget Sound. Leaving the cirque, the opaque, silty gray waters braid past rocky gravel bars where bits of lichen, moss, alders, willows, and a few blooming flowers mark the initial stages of forest succession. Young alders form a thick, almost impenetrable wall along the riverbanks, while older forests of hemlock and silver fir mantle the higher terraces.

Much of the shape and character of the lower Nooksack Valley is also the result of glaciers. Throughout the Pleistocene, glaciers advanced down-valley on numerous occasions. As these glaciers retreated, they left in their wake tons of rocky rubble plucked and carried from the mountains, partially filling the valley floor. Today, the Nooksack River flows over extensive deposits of this debris, transporting small quantities of it downstream, ultimately to the river's estuary on Puget Sound.

The alpine glaciers that linger at the headwater peaks of the Nooksack continue to feed the river, and influence the river's character, temperature, flow, and many other aspects of the river's life, from its fish and wildlife habitat to agricultural and recreational activities.

♦

We woke to a downpour early the next day, and by midmorning we had packed the wet tent and gear and started our way out through dripping alders. By the time we reached the ford where Ruth Creek had washed out the logging road, there was no point in changing into sneakers or rolling our pantlegs: we just marched on through. And, but for the drop in temperature, we were none the wetter.

♦

A mile below the cirque, the Nooksack River leaves North Cascades National Park and enters the Mount Baker–Snoqualmie National Forest. It flows briefly through the Mount Baker Wilderness before entering multiple-use forestland. The Nooksack is still a fast-falling torrent at this point, and cuts a narrow channel down a steep, forested mountain valley, picking up tributary streams along the way. To the south, numerous streams from Ptarmigan Ridge and the extensive glaciers on the north side of Mount Baker wend their way through precipitous canyons in a series of falls and cascading rapids. These join the Nooksack at Wells Creek, just below the dramatic 100-foot cataract of Nooksack Falls.

Trout can be found in pools above this point, but the falls mark the dividing line for the upstream migration of salmon. Below the falls, the Nooksack River system is one of the major salmon-producing streams in the Puget Sound basin. Even though salmon don't reach the headwater streams, there are subtle but important links between the salmon and steelhead, the

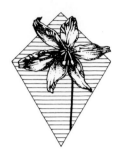

"Even though a river may reach miles above the limits of spawning salmon, feeding eagles, and the nocturnal cavortings of fishers and mink, the fate of these and countless other living members of the watershed community is inextricably linked to the health and productivity of the headwater streams."

eagles that come for them, the deer and elk that winter in the floodplain forests, and the trout, insects, and plants that inhabit the icy headwater torrents. All share in the necessary flow of energy and nutrients, the turbulent flux of water, oxygen, sunlight, and life that is the essence of a living watershed.

◆

Later that summer, on a warm, sunny day in mid-July, I returned to the upper Nooksack on a different kind of trip. I accompanied a small group of students to the meltwater streams of upper Wells Creek. Wells Creek is a headwater tributary of the Nooksack west of Nooksack Cirque, and it drains the northern glaciers and snowfields of Mount Baker. The volcano was striking that day, snow-covered and crisp beneath an azure sky. The sun was warm and the creeks were swollen and noisy.

Dr. David Mason of Western Washington University's Fairhaven College was rummaging around among the river rocks in a tight canyon below a falls. Occasionally he'd smile and hand a rock up to us. We were examining the algae that attach themselves to the rocks, and the many types of insects that feed on and among them. David was explaining the algae's ability to enhance their own environment amid the incredible force of falling water. "My guess, though it's unproven as far as I know, is that the algae that attach to river rocks actually trap river-borne, nonorganic deposits for needed minerals." We found a host of stone fly, caddis fly, and mayfly larvae crowded between and underneath the river rocks. These small aquatic communities common to most headwater streams feed on attached algae, free-flowing plankton, and leaf litter. Biologists think of them in categorical groupings as shredders, collectors, grazers, and scrapers, depending on their function in the food cycle. But whatever their feeding habits, these insects'

adaptations and strategies for survival in this fast-moving and violent world are remarkable. They hold their positions amid the turbulence of flood and meltwater by burrowing, clinging, or simply by being streamlined enough to withstand the flow. Still, many plants and animals are regularly swept downstream by the force of the current, and they in turn provide food for increasingly complex communities of birds, fish, insects, and amphibians that inhabit downstream waters.

David Mason clearly enjoys these high mountain torrents, and though his research into aquatic ecosystems has taken him from the Antarctic to the Arctic, he manages to return to the upper Nooksack year after year. As we stood along the rocky streambank and watched a pair of birds known as dippers work the opposite shore, he explained to us that headwater streams like Wells Creek are considered "producers" in the overall river system. There is a surplus of nutrients in these cold, highly oxygenated and mineral-rich headwater streams, because there are fewer consumers. Downstream, as the numbers of amphibians, large fish, riparian mammals, and birds increase, consumption out strips production. The contribution of nutrients is a valuable function of swift mountain streams, one that is difficult to quantify and not often understood, yet it is an essential part of the finely evolved balance of the watershed system. Even though a river may reach miles above the limits of spawning salmon, feeding eagles, and the nocturnal cavortings of fishers and mink, the fate of these and countless other living members of the watershed community is inextricably linked to the health and productivity of the headwater streams.

Interestingly, scientists are unsure as to how the "primary producers," the algae species, actually got to headwater streams originally, or how they remain there despite the force and persistence of downstream movement. It is one of those small but somehow appropriate mysteries of the river that keep us enchanted, in spite of all we may know.

Historically, headwater streams like Wells Creek and the upper Nooksack were the least affected by development. But with our expanding population and increasing demand for energy and resources, these streams too are now seen as ripe for development. Logging in state and national forests continues to push into higher, steeper, and more marginal territory, and expansion of an active mine is slated soon for Wells Creek. In 1986, the Federal Energy Regulatory Commission (FERC) issued two licenses for additional hydroelectric projects on North Fork Nooksack tributaries; applications are pending for several others.

Although developers and timber interests may be required to take mitigating measures to protect the environment, there is no way to assess the cumulative impact of all of these projects on the watershed as a whole. In response to overwhelming public concern, the Mount Baker–Snoqualmie National Forest has recommended the North Fork of the Nooksack for inclusion in the National Wild and Scenic Rivers System, from its headwaters down to the Highway 9 bridge above Deming. Such a designation would protect not only the recreational qualities of the river system but much of the forest, fish, and wildlife values of the river corridor as well.

Toward late afternoon, as we explored the pools and riffles, a strong, steady breeze rose over Wells Creek and the upper Nooksack. Down-valley, a flock of cliff swallows appeared. They darted back and forth above the creek, honing in with uncanny accuracy on swarms of insects that were lifted and carried by the upstream winds. Some of those unwary insects would be wafted far upstream into the headwater reaches of the Nooksack—some, perhaps, even into Nooksack Cirque. Watching the swallows, I remem-

bered another bird, that high alpinist among songbirds, the gray-crowned rosy finch. Even now, I thought, a rosy finch might be cruising the upper snowfields and glaciers of Nooksack Cirque, where some of these insects might soon come to rest. Delivered by the valley winds and stunned by the cold of the snow and ice, the insects are easy prey for rosy finches. Finches, ice insects, and an assortment of spiders and beetles all depend on these upstream thermal currents and the bugs they carry. These high mountain dwellers, in their own small but necessary way, are also tied to the movement and flow of the watershed cycle.

The swallows danced off beyond a ridge, but the thought lingered. And a taste of the glaciers stayed with me as I followed the creek back out to the road, and continued on downriver.

◆

Fireweed and reflection, Nooksack headwaters, Mount Baker-Snoqualmie National Forest

Methow

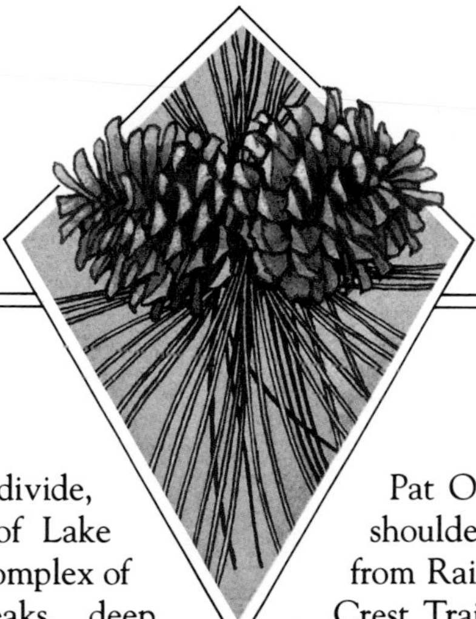

East of the Cascade divide, the country north of Lake Chelan is a remote complex of sheer mountain peaks, deep river canyons, and broad, grassy bottomlands. In the midst of this rugged terrain, the river valleys have an open and inviting character, and year-round accessibility. This combination has made one major river valley, the Methow, a haven for wildlife as well as one of the most popular recreational sites in the state.

The Methow River drains a region where the central Cascades hold back the thrust of Pacific storms and wring moisture from lesser fronts. As a result, dry, open forests of Ponderosa pine and Douglas fir cloak the mountain slopes, and large tracts of lodgepole pine attest to the extensive role wildfire plays in shaping the forest ecology. At higher elevations, such as Rainy Pass on the North Cascades Highway, montane forests are a mixture of west-side and east-side forest types. Spirelike subalpine fir mingle with blue-green stands of Engelmann spruce along the streamsides, near seeps, and in basins; shaggy mountain hemlocks and scattered groves of western larch grow on cooler, shaded slopes.

The cooler slopes seemed to have vanished that mid-July afternoon when photographer Pat O'Hara, two companions, and I shouldered our packs and started north from Rainy Pass. Our route, the Pacific Crest Trail, eventually led to Cutthroat Pass. At the pass, a high gap of rust gray granite and heather, the drone of the wind was cut with the clatter of mountain goat hooves over broken talus. But the wind was cool and welcome, and from there we could look out over converging ridges to the rugged upper limits of the Methow River country. The granite dome of Liberty Bell rose to the south; the jagged ridges and snowfields of Silver Star Mountain filled the eastern horizon; and to the north, the crest of the Cascade Range lifted brokenly to Tower Mountain. Just beyond it lay the pass that would take us to the headwaters of the West Fork of the Methow River. From there, we would continue down seventeen unbroken miles on one of the finest pristine wilderness rivers in the state.

◆

There's much to be said for walking the headwater courses of rivers, and I know of no better way to get acquainted with new country. As your boots follow over the cobbled draws and glacier-smoothed slabs, a deep sense of the slow passage of rock, ice, and water that gave shape to the landscape begins to sink

◆

Opposite: *Early fall, Methow River Valley*
This page: *Ponderosa pine cone*

♦

This page: *Mule deer*

into your bones. Step-kick across remnant snowfields, stopping to drink at snowmelt creeks, or resting at small mountain tarns, you mark your passage by the ebb and fall of the stream down through the water-worn landscape. Traveling on foot with a mountain river, you can feel the life zones change as you pass from meadows and subalpine groves to valley forests. The miles trail off behind you in hours and days, and the slow pace of the river draws you into its timeless reference.

To some the river is the unbridled beauty of a whitewater reach, and the raft-flipping power of hydraulics and standing waves. To others, it is the evening stillness of a pool as a fly line traces a graceful arc over the surface. But to me the river is that age-old music the earth sings to herself as she lifts up and wears down the continents: a bright and joyful music that invites the myriad life forms to dance!

♦

From Cutthroat Pass we followed the Crest Trail past snowfields and talus slopes broken by weathered cliffs. Sparse stands of subalpine larch gave way to shaded slopes where clusters of subalpine firs stood amid dazzling carpets of red heather, spreading phlox, sky-blue speedwell, and bright paintbrush. Below us, the canyons dropped away into wide, U-shaped valleys not unlike those of the Nooksack. Around sixteen thousand years ago, the last southerly advance of the continental ice sheet entered the Methow region from the Northwest. Harts Pass and Glacier Pass at the river's headwaters were low enough to allow lobes of ice to breach the Cascade divide and travel the length of the Methow River valley. The present shape of the valley was largely determined by this last, late glacial advance.

Unlike the mountains west of the crest, however, the Methow country contains very few alpine glaciers today. Instead, the Methow, and its major tributaries—Early Winters, Rattle-snake, and Wolf creeks, and the Lost, Chewuck, and Twisp rivers—depend almost entirely on rain and snowfall for their sources. And by mid-July the last snowpacks were shrinking quickly in the summer heat.

From our camp below Methow Pass, the striking northwest face of Mount Hardy rose in broken cliffs and snow-filled gullies, a looming sentinel above the headwaters of the river. That evening, as I jotted notes and Pat set up his tripod, the last sunlight fell across the central buttress and northwest cliffs of Mount Hardy, lending to its rough textures a fine relief. The snowy talus slopes at its base had fallen into shadow, and a crescent moon floated high in the darkening sky. The wind had died with the sunset, and the sound of mountain water carried up to us and filled the evening with a soft and delicate music.

The next day we followed the snow-melt stream through high open forests. Squirrels chattered incessantly; flocks of chickadees shot through the trees, and bumblebees worked the wildflowers. The river gained in strength as the valley deepened. Trees became taller, and as the valley wound around to the east, the forest opened into wide avalanche meadows. These were sweet with the smell of summer wildflowers—meadow rue, paintbrush, and columbine—and brushed in with low thickets of willow and aspen. To hikers, often closed in beneath trees, avalanche meadows offer welcome views of the surrounding country, and they allowed us to mark our progress by way of nearby peaks.

In the heat of the day, wildlife was scant, but we noted the tracks of mountain goat, bobcat, and deer, as well as a number of smaller animals. And the short, shrill whistles of pikas echoed across the rocky slopes. The Methow Valley is prized for its rich abundance of wildlife, and this has been a prime attraction for recreationists and sportsmen. Most well known,

of course, and most sought after by hunters in the fall, are the valley's resident herds of mule deer.

Mule deer are handsome buff to blue-gray animals with distinctive white breast and rump patches, and long—some would say ungainly—ears. The Methow harbors the largest mule deer population in Washington. Between twenty thousand and thirty thousand of them inhabit the valley. Unlike their black-tailed cousins of the coast, mule deer are herd animals, traveling in bands or groups along their migratory routes.

In summer, mule deer range to the high country meadows of the Methow, such as those we were passing through. They also migrate as far as North Cascades National Park and the Pasayten Wilderness. But as the first snowfalls dust their summer ranges, they retrace

their migration routes along the river corridors of the Twisp, Lost, Chewuch, and Methow rivers to their winter range in the lower Methow Valley. They're easily seen then, grazing the open south slopes, as well as available bottomlands, where they feed primarily on bitterbrush. During times of extreme cold, not uncommon in the Methow country, mule deer will head for the thermal cover offered by old growth forests along the river bottoms. They also return to the rivers in May and June, when they rely heavily on riparian areas for fawning. Here, as in west-side valleys, the combination of dense cover and fresh, abundant browse makes an ideal habitat that is a safe refuge from predators. Later, the deer utilize riparian areas to migrate up-valley to their summer ranges. Obviously, the health and natural condi-

◆

Valley ranch, Chewuch River Valley

tion of the Methow river corridors are essential for the survival of these animals. But while summer range is abundant, increasing development and fencing in the lower river valley has caused and will continue to cause them extreme hardship during a difficult time of year.

White-tailed deer, moose, and black bear also inhabit the valley, and all are, to varying degrees, dependent on riparian areas as well. In the arid forests and brushlands of eastern Washington, the rich, productive habitat found along rivers and streams is all the more critical for wildlife.

The Methow and its tributaries form one of the least disturbed river systems in the state. In the coming years, it will take close cooperation from many management agencies—federal, state, and local—to ensure that the valley's excellent habitat, as well as its opportunities for wildlife-related recreation, are preserved. Natural communities seldom correspond with random political boundaries. Now is certainly none too soon to consider protective measures that will coordinate conservation efforts over all owners and jurisdictions on this watershed.

◆

On our last night out we camped in a grove of old firs along the river. Owls called from the opposite bank, and a nighthawk swooped low over us. We talked of the country, and the river that gives it life. For days our trail had followed the course of the upper Methow—a robust, wild, and splendid mountain stream—but we were at a loss as to why the river hadn't been protected by any of the surrounding Wilderness areas. We all agreed, though, that there could be no more deserving candidate for a designated Wild River in the state. And few unprotected rivers will survive the next generation intact.

There is also reason for concern about the future of important tributaries to the Methow. The Lost River enters the Methow from the north through the spectacular (and trailless) Lost River Gorge, but the lower three miles of the Lost are currently open to development. Farther east, the Chewuch River offers whitewater rafting in spring, and the Twisp, to the south, provides access to the backcountry of North Cascades National Park and Lake Chelan National Recreation Area. Both the Chewuck and Twisp valleys presently contain excellent habitat for wildlife, as well as healthy salmon and steelhead runs, yet hydropower proposals and mining exploration suggest a different scenario for these and other east-side Cascade rivers in the near future.

◆

For well over a century the Methow Valley remained a lonely outpost of small farms and ranches. Civilization had appointments elsewhere. Completion of the North Cascades Highway in 1972 changed that to a degree, but the valley still retains its natural integrity and rustic charm. Today the Methow is poised at the crest of profound change. If plans for a major downhill ski development are realized, the valley could become one of the most heavily developed recreation resorts east of the Cascade crest. The attendant pressures brought upon all of the valley's natural resources would be extreme.

There are few measures available, outside of Wilderness designation, that would ensure that outstanding natural communities, such as those of the Methow Valley, and their vital habitats will survive in the years to come. The Wild and Scenic Rivers Act gives us a great opportunity in the Methow, namely, to protect these narrow corridors that harbor such an abundance of life in this land of little rain.

◆

Opposite: *Methow Pass and Mount Hardy, Methow headwaters, Okanogan National Forest*

This page: *Mountain goat*

Skykomish

The weather was typical for springtime in the Northwest. The sky lay low over the lush green fields of pasture grass that covered the lower Skykomish Valley, and soft bursts of blossoms rested like small clouds on backyard fruit trees. The real clouds were deepening farther up the valley, and a light drizzle at Monroe deferred to a steady rain at Sultan. By the time I stopped for a cup of tea at Gold Bar, fresh snow was plastering the timbered hills above town and the temperature had taken a serious downward turn. Friends had assured me that a raft trip down the famed whitewater of the Skykomish River would be an unforgettable experience, but I'd somehow failed to consider death by hypothermia as part of the excitement. So I consoled myself with the thought that surely no sane person would guide several rafts of novice paddlers down some of the most notorious whitewater in the state in a *snowstorm*, and sipped my tea slowly as the rain beat against steamy plate glass windows.

Whitewater rafting is one of the fastest-growing sports in Washington, but it has yet to achieve here the popularity that it enjoys in California and the Southwest, despite the abundance of fast-moving water that splashes through nearly every corner of our state. A large reason is that the sport is relatively new here and it's just beginning to catch on, but another, not so very small, reason might be days like this. Most of Washington's finest whitewater rivers depend on spring runoff for the increased flows needed for rafting. Typically, runoff peaks in May and June, earlier in years of light snowfall. And, frankly, most springs the weather just isn't that conducive to launching oneself with a rubber raft into a frothing ice water torrent, particularly one that's as likely as not to toss you and your raft head over teakettle into a churning rapid.

These thoughts were still in mind as I turned off Highway 2 toward the take-out point on the river. The rain had eased some. Low clouds hung about the limbs of streamside maples and alders, and the sweet smell of cottonwood drifted down over the high, rolling, jade blue waters. Behind me came the clatter of a blue van as it splashed through several mud puddles to a stop, and the driver, clad in full drysuit and Peruvian wool hat, jumped out and began pulling wetsuits out of the back. I knew immediately that our guide had arrived and the trip was on.

Jerry Michalec is a charter member of that inspired breed of river runners whose enthusiasm for whitewater is thoroughly infectious. In

♦

Opposite: *Rapids and granite, Skykomish State Scenic River*
This page: *Vine maple leaf*

fast water he can barely contain his exuberance, and he is the only man I know whose answering machine greets callers with *"Yeeaaahoo!"* Almost immediately the rain was forgotten as I and ten or eleven other rafters scrambled into wetsuits and packed into the van for our put-in below Sunset Falls. There, donning life jackets and helmets, we piled into two rafts and joined several others in a third for a brief review of paddling techniques and safety precautions. We were urged, one and all, to keep our wits sharpened, and then we were off.

The Skykomish below Eagle, Canyon, and Sunset falls is an exceptionally beautiful river. It cuts down a steep, timbered valley beneath spectacular mountains and high snowy ridges. Lacing past house-sized granite boulders and rocky banks mantled with tall forests of fir and hemlock, its waters rear up in translucent whitewater waves at every turn and bend. Rafters consider it to be the state's premier whitewater river, and the Skykomish was selected in 1977 as the first river in Washington's State Scenic Rivers program.

Once on the river, the cold was forgotten in the rigor of paddling and the excitement of whitewater. The first splashes of icy water that doused us were invigorating. We maneuvered through some smaller riffles and the turbulent waves of Cable Drop Rapid before beaching briefly at the confluence with the North Fork to bail and regroup. An osprey perched by its nest in a weathered snag across the river, while its mate eyed us sternly from another large tree a short distance downriver. Beyond the bird the river fell away into a gallery of huge boulders and dense timber. The series of class three (read "difficult") rapids here includes The Maze, and the submerged rock and gaping hydraulic called Anderson Hole. Just beyond the hole lies the steep, jumbled, rock-studded rapid that has become synonymous with the

Skykomish, the biggest rafting drop in the state: Boulder Drop.

From the safe perspective of shoreline rocks upstream and left of the drop, the powerful hydraulics and immense standing waves were sobering. The river was high, running at well over six thousand cubic feet per second, and the narrow entrance to the rapid was a glassy white tongue of water that curled into a series of reversals, breaking waves, and countless blockading boulders.

Boulder Drop is rated as a class five rapid, the highest class runable in a large raft. Jerry slowly studied the run, and carefully went back over some crucial maneuvers and techniques with us. Then we all joined hands, whooped, and set off into the fray.

For a long moment, our raft seemed poised at the entrance to the rapid, and then all was a confusion of exploding waves, shouted commands, and torrents of water hurling over us. We paddled madly—often finding little more than air beneath one end of the raft or another. One second we "highsided" to one side of the boat as we ran up on a boulder, the next, we shot between converging rocks that I was sure would capsize us. Jerry's voice rose above the din with a "Forward left!" and soon we were safely tucked into an eddy behind a huge boulder. We were only halfway through the drop, but were badly in need of bailing. Also, from this point we could watch the other rafts enter the rapid. If the need arose, we were in a good position to strike out quickly for a rescue.

The second raft shot through in fine form and made the eddy, but the third was pushed forcefully into a boulder called Volkswagen Rock. As its rear tube went down, river water rushed in and immediately the raft was swamped. We threw out lines as the paddlers rushed by us, but they were beyond our reach. Two or three were able to climb back on the raft; the rest bobbed down the swollen river like corks. We set out

in chase. The remainder of our run had a serious intent and we paddled even harder. We soon caught up with the raft, empty again, having literally bucked off all hands in a bottomless hole called Bell's Well. By the time we reached everyone, they were safely on shore.

The boats needed bailing and we were all due for a rest. As our fellow paddlers related their stories—somersaulting off the bottom beneath Bell's Well (a fate charmingly referred to as "recirculating") and the like—they all added up to a first-hand taste of the river's power that I, for one, was happy to have missed. In general, there was a deep gratitude for simply being able to breathe again. Most of the paddlers were apprentice guides, and a "Boulder Drop baptism" was an honorable initiation. For one, it had been her second swim through Boulder Drop! But they

come back to the "Sky" time after time. The magic and excitement, the beauty and power of this swift mountain stream, once tasted, have a way of working themselves into your soul.

As we rested, the clouds suddenly lifted. Across the river the precipitous, snow-streaked summit of Mount Index broke through and for a time dominated the riverscape amid ragged swirls of cloud. Sunlight reflected off gold-green spring leaves rustling around us, and the waves and riffles danced in their whiteness. A pair of mergansers flapped by with obvious business upriver, and I knew that downstream, spring chinook salmon were following suit, working their way from pool to pool in the springmelt torrent.

As a State Scenic River, the Skykomish is protected from impoundments, diversion dams, and harmful developments on state-owned lands along the

♦

Whitewater rafting on the Skykomish River

river. The Washington State Parks & Recreation Commission also coordinates all government agencies that have jurisdiction along the river corridor. This arrangement has already resulted in the redesign of state highway projects along the river to be more compatible with river values. The state has also directed Snohomish and King counties to review their shoreline management plans with an eye toward bringing them in line with state directives. But it remains unclear how—or if—state designation will affect FERC's decision process in siting hydropower dams on State Scenic Rivers. The program has been described by its coordinator as a "gentlemen's agreement" with FERC. Just how long the gentlemen will continue to agree, in the face of pending dam applications, remains to be seen.

While less than ten percent of the South Fork Skykomish flows through U.S. Forest Service lands, nearly all of its tributary streams above Gold Bar are federally controlled. These include the Miller, Beckler, Foss, and Tye rivers, as well as the entire drainage of the North Fork Skykomish above the town of Index.

The Miller and Foss rivers gather in the stunning alplands of the Alpine Lakes Wilderness, western Washington's most accessible and most popular wilderness area. From the high, rock-rimmed lakes and waterfalls, and the glaciers of Mounts Hinman and Daniel, the rivers flow north into steep, forested valleys where elk and deer browse beneath roost trees, and salmon and steelhead ply their lower reaches.

The Beckler River is a major tributary feeding the South Fork Skykomish from the north. Despite heavy logging of the surrounding country, the upper river gorge at Boulder Falls remains rugged and picturesque. Salmon climb nearly to the headwaters of the Beckler to spawn, and fine stands of old growth

forest line the river's banks. As they do on the Miller and Foss, kayakers run the rapids of the lower Beckler and anglers line the banks.

The Tye forms the headwaters of the South Fork Skykomish, and Highway 2 follows its upstream course to Stevens Pass. Fed by the alpine jewels of Tye and Skyline lakes, the upper Tye cuts through a series of steep granite canyons before dropping into the shady forests of the valley.

◆

As we finished lunch, I asked Jerry about boating the North Fork, and his eyes lit up. "Continuous excitement!" He explained that the river features over ten miles of class three and four rapids through splendid old growth forests beneath the six-thousand-foot rise of Gunn Peak. But it's primarily a river for skilled kayakers. "There's just too much whitewater for rafts, and not enough time to bail." Thinking of the chaos of whitewater both inside *and* outside our raft as we raced through the tail waves at Boulder Drop, I was content to take his word for it.

◆

Soon after we put back in, we swept through a series of smaller rapids—The Ledge, Marbleshoot, and Deja Vu—to the Burlington Northern railroad bridge east of the town of Gold Bar. A freight train chugged slowly up the north side of the river, and the rippling waters shimmered in broken sunlight. A few summer homes dotted the shore, and too soon the highway bridge that marked our final takeout appeared beyond a long, southerly bend. After helping with the rafts and gear on shore, I sat against a rock to take some notes. Jerry was just leaving to retrieve the van, still in his emblematic drysuit, and still in excellent spirits. "No need to bother with those notes, Tim," he called out. "You're going to remember this trip for a long time."

◆

Opposite: *Autumn pond, Tye River, Mount Baker-Snoqualmie National Forest*

Wenatchee
River System

The first of the fall rains had begun in earnest, and the foothills around home had taken on those somber tones of damp gray and green that would become all too familiar over the coming months. In spite of the long and unseasonably warm summer that had just slipped past, I wasn't quite ready for the rain, or for the usual autumn tasks that came with it. I knew summer was still lingering east of the mountains, and I knew precisely where I wanted to be.

It wasn't difficult to talk my old climbing partner, Chuck Easton, into a midweek trip to the Wenatchee River country. Chuck had just acquired an older VW camper bus and liked to joke that now, past forty, he was ready to enter "the RV years." He was never too specific as to what this mythical time entailed exactly. All I could tell for certain was that it had more to do with lawn chairs and ice chests than backpacks and dehydrated foods. I also knew that not too many weeks earlier, Chuck had hiked out twenty-two miles with a foot injury from a climbing trip in the Pasayten Wilderness, so the lure of a lazy canoe trip down the lower White River to Lake Wenatchee would not be without its appeal. Two days later we were strapping canoe (and lawn chairs) atop the bus and heading off into the drizzle.

Clouds hung low over the Skykomish Valley, and the mountains were all but hidden. It was a scene reminiscent of an earlier spring trip up that same valley, only this time the clouds weren't spitting snow. But as the highway climbed out of Tye Canyon, patches of sunshine began to break through, and just below Stevens Pass we passed out of the clouds and into the stunning subalpine world of autumn in the high Cascades. Meadows and avalanche fans were burnt red and gold against the sky and the trees were washed in light. We stopped for a breath of mountain air, and started down into the warm clear weather of the Wenatchee Valley.

The free-flowing rivers and forested valleys of the Lake Wenatchee district of Wenatchee National Forest offer a range of recreational uses and seasonal opportunities that are outstanding. The wide array of scenic mountain rivers, and the dazzling blue east-side skies that brighten their pools, are easily reached from the slightly damper population centers of Puget Sound. In like manner, the Wenatchee area's rivers offer a cool mountain respite from the flat summer heat of the eastern part of the state. Couple this with year-round accessibility and unparalleled natural beauty and you

♦

Opposite: *Wenatchee River, Tumwater Canyon*
This page: *Hooded merganser*

"... the whitewater run from Leavenworth to Monitor is easily the most popular run in the state, attracting between sixteen thousand and eighteen thousand boaters annually...."

have a recreational resource unique in all of Washington.

The Wenatchee River system drains the eastern slope of the Cascade crest from the Chiwawa divide in the heart of the Glacier Peak Wilderness, to Mount Stuart at the southern end of the Alpine Lakes Wilderness. It's a country of steep, fast-moving rivers and broad forested valleys. Best known, perhaps, and one of the most striking reaches of whitewater in the state, is the swift torrent of the Wenatchee River where it cuts through Tumwater Canyon above Leavenworth. Although expert kayakers can run this canyon, most whitewater boaters put in well below it at Leavenworth. In fact, the whitewater run from Leavenworth to Monitor is easily the most popular run in the state, attracting between sixteen thousand and eighteen thousand boaters annually.

From Stevens Pass we followed Nason Creek down a sunny corridor lit with flamelike patches of mountain ash and vine maple. At Coles Corner the creek takes a hard bend to the north and so did we. Leaving the highway, we headed toward Lake Wenatchee and the mountain streams that feed it. Highway 2 continues south to follow the Wenatchee River just above the rapids and cascades of Tumwater Canyon. I'd taken that road earlier that summer to raft the big waves of the lower river, but on this particular day I had my mind set on a more contemplative float. The milky meanders of the White River above Lake Wenatchee promised just that kind of trip.

We arrived at the lake late in the day and followed a Forest Service road up the Little Wenatchee River. The Little Wenatchee is a lovely snow-fed stream that threads through some fine stands of old growth forest and offers several excellent riverside camps. Like the White River, its nearest neighbor to the north, the Little Wenatchee feeds into the west end of Lake

Wenatchee and harbors a sockeye salmon run in early fall.

Afternoon sunlight fell softly through golden maples; bright dogwood leaves littered the road. We gathered some wood up-valley and made camp that night along a broad glide of the river. Just upstream, a splendid old forest of Douglas fir and cedar shaded the water, and a fisherman's trail wound beneath the tall fluted columns. Toward evening I listened as a winter wren whistled down the dark.

◆

The sun was high and warm the next morning as we launched our canoe into the White River below its confluence with the Napeequa. The Napeequa flows south out of the mountainous high country of Glacier Peak Wilderness and joins the White River in the open valley at Napeequa Crossing. Of the Napeequa's sixteen-mile length, roads merely brush its lower mile, and trails parallel only another five. It's easy to imagine how this hidden valley inspired its winsome nickname, the "Shangri-la of the North Cascades." A series of large glaciers feeds the Napeequa River, and the White draws from the White River Glacier on the southern massif of Glacier Peak. By fall the meltwater from glaciers is considerably reduced, and the morning presented to us a beautiful translucent green river glimmering beneath the timbered rise of Wenatchee Ridge.

A chorus of robins and varied thrushes rattled the brush as we drifted down the river's slow meanders. The turning October leaves of maples and willows, the burnt orange of mountain ash, and the deep burgundy of red osier dogwood lined the banks, their colors kindling the pools into flame. A family of young mergansers startled up and kept ahead of us the rest of the day, and an old blue heron flapped across an oxbow meander to let us slip by.

We paddled through quiet opaque

waters in sunlight and shadow, rounding sharp bends where broad sandy bars were streaked with otter slides, and following riffles and glasslike pools down shady corridors beneath overhanging cedars. At one bend, an osprey nest atop a stout snag commanded the river upstream and down. At another, a spawned-out sockeye was caught on a downed log, just below the surface. Heron tracks, beaver-chewed trees, the delicate tracks of deer along the river's edge. . .wherever we looked we saw signs of the life of the river, and the slow pace of paddling allowed us to savor them.

Chuck spotted a merganser gulping down a trout, and, later, a small water buttercup flowering beneath the river's surface. As the valley broadened above the lake, the great spreading crowns of cottonwoods were all we saw beyond the brushy banks, those and the far mountain ridges, quiet in the golden light of afternoon.

♦

Year by year, canoeing is slowly catching on in the Wenatchee River country. Both the Little Wenatchee and the Wenatchee River below the lake are favorites, along with the White. Canoeing is a fitting addition to the kinds of family-oriented recreational activities for which the area seems a mecca. Like automobile camping, picnicking, fishing, hiking, nature study, and other activities popular in this area, flatwater canoeing requires few technical skills. Children and oldsters seem equally at ease with a paddle in their hands and a fishing pole leaning over the gunwale. As new parents, my wife and I found ourselves taking the canoe along on family outings over the past summer more often than not. I've a suspicion that trend will continue.

If canoeing has grown in popularity here over the past decade, then whitewater rafting and kayaking have ex-

♦

Osprey with fish, Wenatchee River, Wenatchee National Forest

♦

This page: *Whitewater rodeo, Wenatchee River*

ploded. Among whitewater enthusiasts, nearly all agree that one of the most beautiful as well as exciting runs they know is the Chiwawa River. The litany that usually follows is nearly universal: weather, scenery, wildlife, fun —and a lengthy float through nearly untouched valley forests.

The Chiwawa River flows south for thirty-five miles from the Glacier Peak Wilderness to the Wenatchee River. It lies just east of the Napeequa Valley, separated by Chiwawa Ridge. Its long valley floor is mantled in a stately forest of fir and Ponderosa pine, and graceful cedars stir along the riverbanks. From the river, the wooded shoreline is only occasionally broken by a smooth, high ledge of shale, or a sand cliff riddled with swallow holes. Boaters on the Chiwawa descend nearly continuous rapids through three lovely gorges. And compared to the lower Wenatchee River, the Chiwawa is a veritable wilderness in terms of traffic. Upstream from the put-in at Huckleberry Ford, logjams limit boating, and most rafters take out at the Route 209 bridge. Most days you can count more deer than boaters along this stretch of river.

♦

Paul Sanford has an interesting perspective on the Trinity area and the Chiwawa Valley. Having worked in the Lake Wenatchee district of the Wenatchee National Forest for the past twenty-six years, and having camped, fished, hiked, or paddled in the valley for each of those years, he speaks of the Chiwawa with a note of reverence and wonder in his voice. "You know," he told me when I was able to catch him by phone, "there are families who have been holding reunions on the Chiwawa since the thirties. It's a unique valley for these parts. When I drive that gravel road up the drainage through the big trees, it feels like a scenic wonderland, but it's developed enough—with campgrounds and picnic areas—for families and older people to use. It's totally unlike the White River, where clearcuts and developments can be seen. The Chiwawa's nearly pristine. Even Trinity. It's old and rustic and seems to belong there. And it's a beautiful entrance to the wilderness."

Miners first prospected the Trinity area in the 1880s, but they were by no means the first to visit the valley. The Chiwawa River was an early route for Indian families traveling between eastern and western Washington. Fishing spots and berry fields were as plentiful in the upper valley then as they are now, and an active trade was carried on across the Buck Creek–Suiattle River divide. A large encampment and gathering place was located at the mouth of Chikamin Creek in the lower valley, and by the mid-1800s trappers were also using this site as a stopover on their way up-valley. Miners and homesteaders soon followed, and 1920 saw the last of the seasonal gathering trips by Indian families in the valley. But the farms didn't pay in the lean years that followed, and the homesteaders too went their separate ways. The long tradition of seasonal use in the valley lives on, though.

Only, today, those uses fill most of the year.

As recreation specialist for the district, Paul Sanford doesn't really have a "slack" season anymore. Sunny skies and clear, cold winter days have led to a dramatic increase in winter recreation. It is no surprise that both snowmobilers and cross-country skiers enjoy the corridor roads along the beautiful snowbanked rivers. The Wenatchee National Forest is now arranging with the state as well as with private resort owners to groom over 150 miles of snowmobile and cross-country ski trails in the district. Ski touring around the state park area on Lake Wenatchee has increased from around a dozen to two hundred to three hundred people on a good weekend in recent years. The Little Wenatchee and White Rivers are also popular ski touring routes, and Sanford estimates that thirty to forty people a month make the twenty-five-mile ski trip up the Chiwawa River

Road to the old mining settlement of Trinity. Additional cross-country routes are being developed along the White River, and Kahler and Nason creeks, and the trend shows no sign of abating.

In late spring, as snow leaves the river valleys and the high country melts out, the rivers swell and kayakers and rafters are joined by fishermen in the riverside camps. Steelhead and chinook salmon run late summer in the Chiwawa, sockeye in the Little Wenatchee and White rivers, and rainbow trout and Dolly Varden rise in logjam pools throughout the district. From the rivers, one might catch an occasional trace of smoke from a campfire, but the real crush on the Chiwawa and its sister valleys in the Wenatchee starts on Memorial Day weekend and holds strong through Labor Day.

Families with small children, seniors with travel trailers and RVs, hikers, inner-tubers, berry pickers, and campers are drawn to these clean mountain

◆

Rafters, Chiwawa River, Wenatchee National Forest

rivers as to a shrine. Campgrounds dot the Wenatchee River country from Nason and Icicle creeks to the south, clear around to the Entiat and Mad rivers east of the Chiwawa. The Chiwawa alone hosts fifteen Forest Service campgrounds and provides access to twenty-two trails. Opportunities for dispersed camping and picnicking in secluded spots along the river are virtually unlimited—at least for now.

The Chiwawa is one of only three raftable eastern Washington rivers remaining in a natural state. Future growth projections for the Puget Sound region and other parts of the state are staggering. In less than a generation, recreational demands on rivers throughout the Northwest could more than double, and many relatively unspoiled streams such as Icicle Creek and the Chiwawa, Entiat, and Mad rivers will be prime attractions. As logging and development continue to increase in our national forests, undisturbed rivers like these will become harder and harder to find.

Seeing this, and responding to overwhelming public sentiment, the Wenatchee National Forest has recommended that the Chiwawa, as well as the White, Napeequa, and Wenatchee rivers and Icicle Creek, be included in the National Wild and Scenic Rivers System. To that list, a far-sighted planner might well add the Little Wenatchee, Entiat, and Mad rivers. All are equally deserving and may, in the not-too-distant future, be just as badly needed.

♦

That evening, after our canoe trip, Chuck and I drove east from the White River and made camp on a quiet bend on the Chiwawa. A ribbon of wood smoke drifted out over the stream to mingle with the autumn stars and the sound of flowing water ran low and clear. Beyond the fire, we could see a last misty glimmer of riverbank off to the west beneath the darkened wall of Chiwawa Ridge. It was that slow time of year in the mountains, between the last of summer and the fall hunt, and we had the campground—possibly the whole valley—to ourselves. After arguing good-naturedly over which end of the canoe did more paddling that day, Chuck turned the talk toward his youth.

In those days, when his parents took him out camping in the Cascades, along rivers, beneath the old trees, it wasn't unusual to have a campground to yourself, even in summer. "It hadn't really caught on back then. It was canvas tents and the station wagon, hot dogs on a stick. . . but the woods were everywhere, and the rivers were all like this." Below us, a driftwood pile shone silver in the twilight, and the far bank was softened with the faint glow of dogwood leaves. Chuck added a stick to the fire, and settled back with a fresh cup of tea. "Yes, McNulty," he continued—never one to end on a somber note—"now that the RV years are upon us, we're going to need all these river valleys we've got."

♦

Opposite: *"Shangri-la,"* *the Napeequa Valley, Glacier Peak Wilderness*

Cispus

It was a warm, sunny day in mid-June when some friends and I carried two rafts down a steep bank to a put-in on southwest Washington's Cispus River. The snowmelt rush of opaque gray-green water tugged at low-hanging branches. *"Come on,"* it said. *"We've got places to go!"* I still had to shuttle a car down to the other end of our run, and I wasn't at all sure the river wanted to wait for that. I didn't.

Originating in the meadowlands and snowfields of the Goat Rocks Wilderness and the glacier-clad slopes of Mount Adams, the Cispus River flows west unchecked to its confluence with the Cowlitz, a mile above Cowlitz Falls. Its fifty-mile course through un- broken forests and meadowlands roughly parallels the larger Cowlitz River to the north, which in turn feeds the Columbia. I'd known the Cispus only as the site of the Cispus Environmental Center, and nothing prepared me for the sheer liquid beauty of the valley. As we put in I watched the emerald rise of Blue Lake Ridge recede in the clear mountain sky, then saw a hawk circle far up-valley. An icy splash of water brought me back around, and we were off.

The upper Cispus is a narrow mountain stream, and our rafts threaded past small cobbled islands strewn with silvery gray driftwood logs. A small waterfall splashed down to our left, and a pair of dippers skimmed along from rock to rock beside us. The low spreading limbs of shoreline conifers were lit from below with reflected sunlight. Drifting beneath them was like slipping through an aquatic cave lit with lamps of jade. Along the shaded banks, the white blossoms of salmonberry and ox-eye daisies flickered above us like candles.

The river cut its way through mossy, rock-walled gorges hung with lacelike fronds of maidenhair fern and pale blooms of Lewisia. Occasionally, as our rafts came around a bend, the stillness of the forest would erupt into the rustling turmoil of a whitewater rapid. At other times, after bailing, we would look up and see the mountain valley open up like another world.

Midway on our float down the Cispus, the steep curving slope of Tongue Mountain rose above the trees to the west, and the river meandered into a broad cobbled channel. A few miles farther down-valley, Tower Rock looms over the forests and pasturelands of the central valley like a northern El Capitan.

The Tower Rock area is perhaps the most striking part of the Cispus Valley. The peak, an ancient volcanic remnant, is located almost centrally between the surrounding vol-

◆

◆

This page: *Calypso orchids*

canoes of Rainier, Adams, and St. Helens, and its steep north face rises quite dramatically more than two thousand feet above the river valley. Historic reports tell of a Cowlitz Indian village site located in the broad open meadows below the peak, and a large cave in the vicinity recently excavated by archaeologists yielded spear points, microblades, and other hunting tools that date back more than seventy-five hundred years. Other sites in the Cispus Valley have yielded comparable dates. There may be over a dozen sites along the Cispus alone, and they show evidence of continued human use to less than one hundred years ago, about the time the first white settlers arrived.

◆

Deep forested valleys, plentiful wildlife, and a wealth of salmon-producing rivers nurtured this long history of human use in the region. As early as eight thousand years ago, small bands of hunter-gatherers were visiting the Cowlitz, Cispus, and other tributary valleys. One of the oldest trails across the Cascade divide crossed the range north of White Pass. From there, the Cowlitz-Yakima Trail, as it's now called, followed the Cowlitz Valley downstream to the vicinity of Mossy Rock on the lower river. East of the crest, the route descended Summit Creek to the Tieton River.

Along the Cowlitz's headwaters, at the confluence of Clear Fork and the Ohanapecosh River, archaeologists have found the remains of a seasonal village. Artifacts show that the site was used extensively for fishing as well as hunting and huckleberry gathering. Even today, a few residents of the valley remember stories their grandfathers told of Yakima people loading heavy baskets of dried salmon and berries onto their ponies and starting back across the divide as recently as the early 1900s. The dust stirred by these pack trains settled over older campsites that date back from five hundred to fifteen hundred years ago.

Higher, in what is now the Goat Rocks Wilderness, archaeologists have discovered an obsidian quarry site. Obsidian is a black volcanic glass that chips down into fine, sharp projectile points and blades. It was valued by hunting people all across North America, and obsidian from this site was traded as far west as the present town of Randle. Radiocarbon dating of the quarry site shows it was used six thousand years ago.

Dates such as these tend to warp our sense of time. "History" in the Northwest covers a span of a mere two centuries. The thought that human communities were living, traveling, and trading in the Cascade valleys continuously for the past six millennia gives us pause—as it should. We may never know just who these people were, or what their values and beliefs, but in their passing they left behind bits and pieces of their lives. By studying these, in relation to the landscapes in which they're found, we might glean something of the world these people knew. And if those elders from a distant branch of our human family have something to teach us, it's likely to be found in these wild and untrammeled valleys, places not yet thoroughly transfigured by our own overriding view of the world.

Throughout the Cowlitz watershed, the river valleys are dotted with these prehistoric sites, most of them unexplored. In the Cispus Valley one can still find peel scars on old cedars where bark was taken for baskets, clothing, and rope. But just a few miles downstream from the Cispus River's confluence with the Cowlitz, all traces of early use of the valley come to an end beneath the impounded waters of Riffe Lake. Inundated are over fifteen miles of low-elevation valley bottom that may contain some of the most revealing archaeological sites in the Cowlitz system.

The Mossy Rock and Mayfield dams were constructed in the 1950s and 1960s

by Tacoma City Light. The dams were built—without fish passages—over the opposition of the Washington State Department of Fisheries, the state legislature, and a majority of the state's voters. In compensation, the utility was required to fund construction of a large hatchery on the Cowlitz that was to supplant the lost runs of wild salmon. The story that followed was a sad one for the Cowlitz salmon. Epidemic disease and repeated failure to meet quotas drastically reduced the Cowlitz runs. A program of trucking spawning fish around the dams was abandoned in 1979, and the upper Cowlitz basin remains empty of its most valued resident, the wild salmon.

In the Sahaptin tongue the word Cowlitz means "holder of the medicine spirit." Upstream from the slack water of Riffe Lake, the forest closes back in over the river. Eagle roost trees lean over the sparkling riffles and spawning gravels, and fall rains continue to deepen the pools. If there is one thing we can learn from the salmon's magnif-

icent natural history, it's that where the habitat survives, there's always the hope that the salmon can return. And in the Cowlitz basin, it would be difficult to find a more ideal habitat than the Cispus River.

Along with salmon, the early people took deer, rabbits, grouse, elk, and mountain sheep from this valley. Today, the forests of the Cispus continue to harbor elk and deer, as well as spotted owls and mink. Resident cutthroat and rainbow trout still draw the hardiest of fishermen to this wild stretch of river and the bottomlands below Adams Fork continue to provide excellent winter range. Not surprisingly, such natural abundance brings thousands of river users to the valley each year. Camping, picnicking, fishing, hiking, hunting, and berry picking are popular uses now, as they have been for centuries. Located within two to three hours of major population centers in two states, and virtually at the portal of the Mount St. Helens National Volcanic Monument, over-

◆

The Palisades, basalt columns, above the Clear Fork, Cowlitz River, Gifford Pinchot National Forest

night use of the valley has nearly doubled since 1982. Among the fastest-growing recreational activities on the Cispus is whitewater boating, and I can recommend no better way to get a good taste of this lovely valley.

◆

There's a magic to the open valley of the Cispus below Tower Rock. The river broadens and meanders through lush bottomlands, and the looming presence of the peak dominates the view. In the late nineteenth century, miners and homesteaders followed the old Indian trails here. In the 1930s the Tower Rock area was the site of a large Civilian Conservation Corps camp. Today that site houses the Cispus Environmental Center, where each year hundreds of young people are introduced to the beauty and mysteries of the natural world. Not far away a small community of ranches and homes shares the valley with seasonal visitors.

As we continued our float along a flat stretch of the Cispus, and occasional campsites appeared in small openings among the trees, I thought about the many uses people have found for this remarkable valley. The fact that it has remained in so natural and undisturbed a state, in the midst of intensive logging and development in surrounding valleys, speaks well, I thought, not only for the people here, but for the haunting beauty of the valley itself. My reverie remained only half-spun however. It was cut short by the oncoming rush of Smoothrock Falls.

Our boats took the thrilling four-foot plunge of the falls in their flexible, buoyant way, and we turned to look back at the smooth lip of curling water that spanned the river. It was our biggest drop of the day, and it was over all too soon. I suggested we portage back around to have another run at it, but no one took me seriously. So we coasted on downriver to our takeout.

A short distance downstream from Smoothrock Falls is a site the Army Corps of Engineers has identified as a suitable location for a 225-foot-high dam. The dam would impound 94,000 acre-feet of water a good distance up-valley. This is the second project the Corps has proposed for the Cispus. Just downstream of the Iron Creek Campground, another project would back 300 feet of water over some of the most splendid old growth forests in the lower valley. Fortunately, no utilities have yet taken the Corps up on these ideas, but they remain in the *National Hydroelectric Power Study,* page 272, table 1. In the meantime, the entire upper Cowlitz watershed has been flooded with a rash of small-head hydroelectric applications. On the Cispus River, as of this writing, the Federal Energy Regulatory Commission has received five permit applications. The proposed projects would remove 80 percent of the flow from nearly twenty-five miles of the upper, middle, and lower river, and initiate major construction of roads, pipelines, penstocks, powerhouses, and transmission lines. One needn't stretch the imagination to picture what this would do to the nature of the Cispus Valley.

In its forest plan, the Gifford Pinchot Nation-

◆

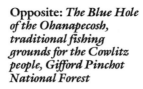

Opposite: *The Blue Hole of the Ohanapecosh, traditional fishing grounds for the Cowlitz people, Gifford Pinchot National Forest*

This page: *Elk*

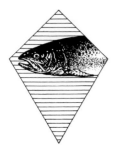

"... our lifetimes may indeed be the eleventh hour for our great rivers... the rivers we fail to set aside now may not be there for the next generation."

al Forest has recommended the Cispus for inclusion in the National Wild and Scenic Rivers System. The Cispus was also listed on the 1980 National Heritage Conservation Recreation Service List as a potential Wild and Scenic River. A recent review of all Washington rivers placed the Cispus on the candidate list for Washington's Scenic River program, and it was included in the Northwest Power Planning Council's Protected Area Program. In short, there should be no question as to the best future use of this remarkable river.

◆

In the early fall of that same year, after the first rains, I returned to the Cowlitz watershed, visiting an archaeological site located a couple of miles below the mouth of the Cispus. My companion that day was Roger Harpel, a river activist deeply concerned about the fate of the entire Cowlitz system. We parked on a logging road and followed a cat track down into the Cowlitz Canyon a couple of miles below the mouth of the Cispus. There, grown over with trees and brush, is the site of

an old fishing village. The Koap site, as it is known to the Cowlitz people, has turned up signs of continual human use dating back thirty-five hundred years before the present.

The milky gray flow slackened as it approached Riffe Lake. The sky was low and overcast, and a cool wind blew up the gorge. The sound of a waterfall carried to where we sat on a rock lip perched over the river. It wasn't hard to imagine the Old Ones pulling big salmon up onto those smooth, gray, river-carved rocks. Roger explained the spray paint marks along the rock walls, the survey stakes, the dimensions of the new Cowlitz Falls dam that would further impound the rolling flow of the river. More power for export to another region. More habitat lost, and another reservoir backing water a mile or two up the lower Cispus River.

As we watched the water flow past the empty rock ledges, it occurred to me that our lifetimes may indeed be the eleventh hour for our great rivers, that the rivers we fail to set aside now may not be there for the next genera-

tion, and that an unspoken yet sacred trust that has existed between man and river for as long as our kind has thrived in this region, will be no more.

That evening found us in headwaters country, where the Muddy Fork splashes down into the swift mountain torrent of the Cispus. Its narrow, rocky course was edged in fern and mosses, and the old forest extended back into the high reaches of the Cascades. Roger told of bringing his four-year-old son to this place so the music of the singing river can find its way into the

boy's young heart. His fight to save the Cowlitz has been a difficult uphill battle, but for the Cispus he has great hope. He spoke with enthusiasm about the effort to stop the hydro projects and gain permanent protection for the Cispus River. We stood silently for a while. The evening sky began to fade, and the wind rustled among the dry willow leaves.

"Yeah," he said after a long pause, "they'll have to wrestle me in public for this one."

White Salmon

Rising abruptly in rounded cliffs over the slack waters of the Columbia River, the Columbia Gorge is one of the most striking landforms in the Pacific Northwest. Carved by the great river as the Cascade Range rose upward some six million years ago, it was the route through which Lewis and Clark first breached that mountain barrier, and today it remains a major corridor between the coast and the interior. To the north, the lava walls of the Gorge are cut by only a handful of rivers that spill down from the Cascade peaks: the Washougal, the Wind, the White Salmon, the Klickitat, and several lesser streams. When legislation creating the Columbia River Gorge National Scenic Area was passed in 1986, portions of these latter two rivers—the White Salmon and Klickitat— were designated National Scenic and Recreational Rivers. For the White Salmon, designation marked the culmination of a decade-long campaign on the part of local residents to save the river from intensive industrial development.

Born among the glaciers and snowfields of Mount Adams, and fed year-round by a network of underground springs, the White Salmon River flows through forests, farmlands, and a steep, rugged gorge of its own to its confluence with the broad reach of the Columbia. The south-tending valley of the White Salmon lies midway through the Cascade Range, where it is influenced by both west-side and east-side climates and vegetation. The result is a rich, complex, and unique botanical habitat. A recent survey of the mid-valley river corridor alone revealed the presence of twenty-one species listed on the Washington Natural Heritage Program's Threatened and Endangered Plant list, including three endemic to the Columbia Gorge and numerous others that are usually found much farther west. This botanical diversity helps make the White Salmon River gorge the memorable setting that it is, hung with ferns and wildflowers along the river and forested with sturdy stands of oak and fir at its higher reaches. Though the valley has been farmed for well over a century, the river corridor itself has remained surprisingly undisturbed.

◆

Esther Schmidt sat in the living room of her Trout Lake farmhouse playing with two young grandchildren and talking about her life on the White Salmon. She recalled going on picnics with her family along the river as a little girl, picking the tart huckleberries that grew along the riverbank. And she re-

◆

Opposite: *White Salmon River Canyon*
This page: *Mule deer*

◆

Opposite: *The road to Goldendale, Klickitat River Valley*

membered the "wonderful experience" of emerging from the trees and seeing the broad volcanic cone of Mount Adams hovering cloudlike over the valley. "I can remember thinking the White Salmon was such a beautiful river. At that time my family lived in the Washougal Valley west of here, and I had no idea I'd be spending my adult life alongside the White Salmon," she said. "I have Leon to thank for that."

Her husband, Leon Schmidt, was out in the barn for the evening milking, and as we talked, the soft lowing of cows drifted across the wide pasture and yard. The Schmidt family had lived in the White Salmon Valley for five generations, Esther told me. Leon grew up on the family farm and Esther has spent some thirty-five years there, helping manage the farm and raising a family. The valley has changed very little over that time. The small farming communities of Trout Lake and Husum still nestle among pasturelands and woods. Elk and deer still filter down out of the surrounding mountains to winter along the river bottoms, and eagles continue to gather along the lower river for the winter salmon runs.

Esther likes to walk with her grandchildren down to where the river flows past the farm, just as she once did with her children. "The river really does have an emotional and spiritual value to me, " she told me. "Sometimes I go walking there just to work off a worry."

Esther Schmidt's worries took a sharp turn for the worse in 1976 when she picked up a copy of the *White Salmon Enterprise*. The headline that particular day announced that her county Public Utility District had released plans to build seven dams on the White Salmon River. One, a mile-wide earthen-fill dam, was to be constructed right above her own community of Trout Lake. "I never thought of myself as an environmentalist, but I became one!" Esther explained how she and several of her neighbors in Trout Lake made an effort to educate them-

Orchard in fall, White Salmon National Scenic River

selves about dams and land-use issues by attending workshops, reading books and government reports, and asking lots of questions. Before long she found she had a common alliance with a "younger generation" of settlers who had arrived in the valley in the late sixties and early seventies. "The developers called them 'hippies,'" she said with a chuckle, "but, by and large, they were industrious, quite well educated, and no strangers to political process. I think all of us in the valley owe a lot to those young people."

Soon, the newly formed Friends of White Salmon began to organize opposition to any additional hydroelectric development on the river. Through open public meetings, informational hand outs, and letters to the editor, the organization explained its position: The White Salmon River already had one dam on its lower reaches; the Conduit Dam and Northwestern Lake provided electric power to growing towns along the Columbia Gorge. Let the White Salmon be a true "multiple use" river by allowing the free-flowing portion of the river to support other kinds of uses. Friends of White Salmon, many of its members having moved there from developed urban areas, envisioned another type of economic future for the valley, one more in keeping with the traditional agricultural, and recreational uses it already experienced. "It wasn't only the river's future that was at stake, we saw the future of farming in the valley threatened by the PUD," Esther added. "We had to do something."

◆

Dennis and Bonnie White were part of the younger generation Esther had spoken of. They moved to the valley in the early seventies and Dennis took a job teaching science in their local school. Both were instrumental in organizing Friends of White Salmon, and both remain active in river conservation issues today. Over an impromptu lunch of cheese and fresh sliced apples from their organically farmed orchard, Dennis sketched in for me their efforts to save the river. "Friends of White Salmon was totally a volunteer organization," he explained, "and each participant contributed in his or her own personal way. There were committees focused on fund-raising, research, economics, and such, and we sponsored a whole series of car washes, auctions, T-shirt sales, a booth at the county fair . . . you name it."

Friends of White Salmon tried to take a long-range view of the valley. They emphasized the attributes the river presently possessed and suggested how those might contribute to the local economy in the future.

"Back then, besides fishing," Dennis continued, "recreational use of the river consisted of kids on inner tubes and a few kayakers. Today, the White Salmon is known as one of the premier whitewater boating rivers in the state. There are at least two professional guiding services in the valley now, and five bed and breakfast establishments have sprung up." He had to smile and shake his head in retrospect. "Even we 'visionaries' couldn't have foreseen this kind of popularity!"

The efforts of Friends of White Salmon, and others who had come to know the river, paid off in success. Although it took ten years, the dams were defeated and the White Salmon received permanent protection through its inclusion in the National Wild and Scenic Rivers System. From the community of BZ Corner downstream to the head of Northwestern Lake, the river has been classified as Scenic and is free to roll through its whitewater gorge undisturbed. The river above BZ Corner, including the reach that flows past the Schmidt farm, is being studied by the Forest Service for possible inclusion in the system as well.

A good idea?

I asked Esther, and Leon when he came back in from the milking. Their answer? An unqualified "yes!" "It's the only way we can keep our rivers from being maligned," Esther explained. "I've seen too many rivers dammed, and blighted, and developed to death. John Muir was right. He said too many people worship the dollar!" Her advice for others working to protect free-flowing rivers throughout the state? "Well, it takes time and dedication. You have to keep yourself informed and well organized, and you have to work tirelessly, sometimes day after day. Most of all, you have to be a long-term runner." She picked up the younger of her two grandchildren and held him on her lap. "But the rewards are worth it."

"Friends of White Salmon. . . envisioned another type of economic future for the valley, one more in keeping with the traditional agricultural and recreational uses it already experienced."

Soleduck

Roy Bergstrom isn't a tall man, and I guessed that might have given him the advantage. I was just barely keeping up as we ducked beneath vine maples and scrambled over logs and boulders in the woods that bordered the Soleduck River. It was a chill morning in late January, and Roy was concerned about the river level. "If it really froze up in the headwaters and the river's too low," he called back to me, "those steelhead are going to be hard to catch." At the time, I was less concerned about catching steelhead than I was about catching Roy. Up ahead I spotted his red-checked hunting cap and fur-collared army coat dropping over a rise. By the time I reached him, Roy was already wading out into the river and unhooking a hammered nickel spoon from his rod. Upstream, a rapid broke into a deep, shimmering hole, and blue water purled against a bank of shale.

At seventy-nine, Roy Bergstrom was in his element.

"Now, when the water's this low," Roy said as he reeled his first exploratory cast back across the channel, "those steelhead don't like to wait around in the holes. They move right on up the river." He cast again and let his lure search lower across the glide, then added

"This may be a tough one today."

I explored the riverbank as Roy worked his way carefully upstream, as deliberate as a scholar paging through a Latin text. A fine mist rose among the tree-tops, and the low limbs of alders shone silver against the dark, moving water. Downstream, the first sunlight hit the far bank, casting a golden sheen over the river as it coursed around a bend and disappeared among the winter trees.

This was the middle Soleduck, well down-stream from Salmon Cascades and Olympic National Park. It's a river Roy knows well. For nearly fifty years Roy has fished this stretch of water for the Olympic Peninsula's prized win-ter steelhead—that magnificent sea-run trout that draws thousands of sport fishermen to coastal rivers like the Soleduck each year. Steelheading has become a significant part of the economy on the Peninsula, but Roy re-members a time when wild steelhead were less than prized by sport fishermen. They were hardly even fished.

"You couldn't believe the roads out here in the thirties and forties," Roy told me as he stopped to change a lure. "Why, they were so narrow and rutted you had to *dodge* the stumps. And the mud and the snow . . . oh cripes!" Beginning in 1941, Roy dodged the

◆

Opposite: *First snowfall, Soleduck River, Olympic National Forest*
This page: *Steelhead*

◆

Steelhead fishing,
Soleduck River, Olympic
National Forest

stumps out to the Peninsula's west end on a weekly basis. His job with the Federal Manpower Commission kept him shuttling between the big logging camps in the Soleduck Valley, where manpower in those wartime years was always in short supply, and Seattle, where a work force could be found. "At $1.05 an hour for a choker setter, you can imagine the turnover," Roy laughed. "They were always looking for new men."

The small community of Sappho was still a booming logging camp in those days, and Roy recalled that the foreman of the operation would always offer him a warm place to stay and a big "logger's breakfast"—steaks, biscuits, stacks of hotcakes, bowls of fruit—with the crews in the morning. "Then they'd all climb onto flatcars and head off to the logging site," he told me. "I'd follow the tracks out to the trestle over the river and fish." Steelhead lay thick in the holes then, and Roy remembers the time he and a friend landed a large female while lying on their stomachs on a trestle to fish under the bridge. "There were pilings and logging cables strewn all over. I don't know how we landed it. But you know," he recalled with a wistful smile, "I never saw *anyone* fishing the river for steelhead back then. Just me, and whatever friends I brought along." He was the proverbial kid in a candy store.

Things changed dramatically for Roy and the west end of the Pensisula in 1951, with the notorious Forks Burn. Wildfires licked across the landscape at a rate of eighteen miles in six hours, and over thirty thousand acres of timberland burned. In the burn's aftermath, logging crews from Oregon, Idaho, and British Columbia were brought in to salvage the timber. As Roy recalls it, "Once those Oregon fellows got a look at the Soleduck and other west end rivers, they came back with their McKenzie River drift boats and really started fishing." Steelheading was immensely popular in Oregon at the time, and it was soon to become so on the pristine rivers of the Olympic Peninsula as well. The Soleduck River was about to gain regional, if not national, notoriety.

◆

The Soleduck has often struck me as the most beautiful of the Olympic Peninsula's many west-side rivers. Its clear snow-fed waters meander in riffles and pools past miles of wooded shoreline, valley farms, and the gathered flows of countless tributary streams. If there's a correlation between natural beauty and biological richness in the Northwest, then the Soleduck presents an excellent case. It is singly the most productive fishery stream on the Peninsula, itself a land of excellent fishery streams. Impressive runs of all Pacific salmon species, as well as steelhead and resident trout, utilize the Soleduck.

Olympic National Forest classified the Soleduck fishery as "outstandingly remarkable" in its forest plan. This is not an overstatement.

I asked Jeff Cederholm, a fisheries scientist for Washington's Department of Natural Resources who has done extensive work on the western Olympic Peninsula, just what it is that makes the Soleduck so special. "It's a combination of a lot of things," Cederholm told me. "The rapids and pools, excellent spawning gravels, an abundance of animal life, and the high quality of the riparian forests . . . all those large trees structuring the aquatic habitat. The Soleduck's not heavily riprapped and built up like other west end rivers. And the natural setting is fabulous." Mark Mobbs, environmental biologist for the Quillayute tribe—whose reservation occupies the river mouth—echoed this assessment. When I questioned him, he emphasized the significant portion of the Soleduck River that is accessible to spawning salmon and steelhead, what biologists refer to as a stream's "anadromous reach." "The Soleduck has a long length for a coastal river," he told me, "and maybe sixty-five miles of anadromous reach. That's quite a bit of habitat, and if you figure in the tributary streams you can almost double that mileage. The river's tributaries in particular are extremely productive salmon habitats. One of them, Lake Creek, has the highest number of redds [spawning sites] per mile in the state." Still, both biologists advised caution. This kind of richness is by no means immune from the kinds of problems associated with habitat degradation on other Northwest rivers.

◆

By midmorning, Roy and I had seen lots of excellent habitat—we were fishing Roy's third "spot" on the river— but no steelhead. Roy explained how pressures have increased on the Soleduck's wild steelhead runs over the years. The tribal fishery harvests the fish commercially at the river mouth,

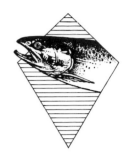

"If there's a correlation between natural beauty and biological richness in the Northwest, then the Soleduck presents an excellent case."

◆

Opposite: *Morning fog in the Ancient Forest, Soleduck Valley, Olympic National Park*

This page: *Avalanche lily in rain, Soleduck headwaters, Olympic National Park*

and sport fishermen and guides using drift boats have become, in Jeff Cederholm's words, "extremely effective." A steelhead hatchery using native stock has begun operation on the river to supplement the declining runs, but Roy sees little similarity between the hatchery products and native fish. As we worked a stretch of river by his old stomping grounds at Sappho, Roy described landing a wild steelhead at that spot the last time he fished it.

"I made the cast and, for a split second, I thought I was hung up," he said. "I picked up my line and in that instant that steelhead was *airborne* down the river. I finally turned him down there by those rocks, and I worked him back and landed him right up here. . . . What a fight." Inevitably, when Roy talked about fishing, it was in the voice of a much younger man. He looked at me straight on as if to convey something of the utmost importance, and said, "*That* was excitement!" He waded back out into the drift and tried an-

other cast, then turned and added, "There's nothing like those natives. Hatchery fish can't compare with them; they just don't have the fight." Then he frowned and said, "They been eating too much dog food!" and he picked up and moved down the river.

A high overcast was blowing in over the valley, harbinger of another rain. Roy had told me earlier that he never caught fish at noon, and the morning was slipping past. As I followed him, an eagle dropped from a spruce just below us. We watched as it crossed the river and flapped off through the winter bottomlands. Then Roy turned and took a last look back up-valley. I had the sense that he was looking back, too, on all the days and years he'd come here to fish, the stories he'd told and the memories this sparkling water brought back to him.

"Isn't this a fine stretch of water?" he asked at last. And, fish or no fish, it was.

Dosewallips

The small creature seemed to materialize out of the duff and needles of the forest floor. I didn't move as it bounded across the trail, scampered onto a downed log, and stood on its hind feet to watch me. There was no mistaking the high rounded ears, the reddish-brown coat, and golden throat patch. It was a marten, and it seemed as astounded as I was. For a brief moment, time stood still. Then the marten broke the spell by moving to a safer distance, a short way up a tree where it stopped to look again. Another two blinks and its sleek form slipped off down the timbered slope toward the white rush of the Dosewallips River.

Martens have become rare and are seldom seen in the Olympic Mountains. Like their cousins the fishers, who are believed to have disappeared from the Olympics, martens seem to prefer the rich old growth forests of the river valleys. In nearly twenty years of tramping Olympic trails, I've spotted only two. Both were in old forests alongside rivers, and both were in the wild and rugged valleys of the eastern Olympics.

◆

The east side of the Olympic Peninsula is in many ways a country unto itself. High broken ridges and prominent peaks frame the eastern ranges. Unlike the sedimentary mountains of the interior and western Olympics, the tough basalt bedrock of the east Olympics yielded less to Ice Age glaciers. As a result the east-side rivers are incised into narrow, steep-sided valleys. Rivers like the Gray Wolf, Dungeness, Quilcene, Dosewallips, Duckabush, Hamma Hamma, and Skokomish begin in high mountain snowfields and meadows, and descend in sheer, short, rocky courses to the waters of the Strait of Juan de Fuca and Hood Canal.

Since much of the eastern range drops off abruptly into tidewater, early settlement of the east Olympics was confined to the shoreline of Hood Canal and the lower portions of the valley floors. As a result, the area retains much of its natural character. Small communities and rural farms share the land with a rich diversity of fish, wildlife, and forests. Like the Cascades in microcosm, the interior ranges of the Olympic Mountains also trap moisture from Pacific fronts. This has created an arid "rainshadow" in the northeast Olympics, and tempered rainfall along much of the eastern front as well. This, combined with the area's proximity to the population centers of Puget Sound, has helped make the east Olympics an increasingly popular recreation area suitable for day trips and weekend jaunts. The

◆

Opposite: *Boulders, moss, and leaves, Dosewallips River*
This page: *Roosevelt elk*

Dosewallips Valley alone supports two campgrounds and a state park, and provides access to the wilderness trails of Olympic National Park.

I should confess, the east Olympics are "backyard" country for me, and attachments run deep. Memories and events mingle with places to become part of a richly woven personal landscape, one that overlays the natural world and brings it closer. Friendships and seasons, moments of vision and long days of work in the rain all deepen one's ties to a place. Some encounters find their way into poems. Others come back unexpectedly when my wife, Mary, and I visit a favorite place along a lakeshore or stream. But all are held and nourished within that singular ebb and passage of time that finds its closest metaphor in the flow of the river.

♦

Of the many clear rivers that thread the forested canyons of the east Olympics, best known and most popular among recreationists of all stripes is the Dosewallips. Hikers know the Dosewallips headwaters country as among the most scenic in the Olympics: rocky, snow-covered peaks break into rolling meadowlands strewn with wildflowers and quick, ribbonlike streams. Anglers, campers, and picnickers all have favorite spots along the river as well. One large attraction for those who know the Dosewallips country is its resident herd of migratory elk. From the small bands of the subalpine meadows to the winter herds browsing among the lower valley bottoms, the elk are as much a part of this river valley as the head-

water peaks, snowlit above the evening shadows.

No animal is more symbolic of the Olympic wilderness than the Roosevelt elk. Named for the president who, in 1909, set aside the Mount Olympus National Monument to preserve its habitat, the elk also figured strongly in the 1938 Act of Congress that created the national park. Most of the east Olympics and much of the Dosewallips Valley, however, are outside the national park, and the east-side herds must leave the park to winter in the lower valleys. In the past, elk numbers in the east Olympics kept pace with the level of development and activity in the lower valleys. However, in recent years, the rate of logging and development has increased dramatically, and some managers fear this might affect the long-term viability of elk and other east Olympic wildlife populations. A study conducted in 1985 noted that the number of residences in the Dosewallips and Duckabush valleys increased from about fifty to two hundred and fifty over the past three decades. Forty percent of the national forest lands in these valleys had been logged by that time, as had 80 percent of the privately owned timberlands. The study also demonstrated that elk tend to avoid human activities in the Dosewallips and Duckabush valleys, notably road traffic and permanent residences, and suggested that continued development of these lower valleys would undoubtedly affect the herds.

For the past twenty-seven years, Mike Ragon has been an agent for Washington's Department of Wildlife in the area. He views the effects of logging and subdevelopment on wildlife as being cumulative in nature, but they may quickly become acute during a severe winter. Ragon remembers the winter of 1968–69, when the east Olympic valleys were totally snowbound. "You could barely get up the valleys that winter," he told me. "There were eighteen inches to two feet of snow at Brin-

♦

This page: *New friends
and old, Valley Forest,
Gray Wolf River,
Olympic National Forest*

Overleaf: *Sunrise,
Dosewallips Estuary,
Dosewallips State Park*

non, and it deepened as you went up-valley. The elk survived all right, but a good bit of the areas that were used as winter range that year have houses on them now. The influx of people into the area, and the increase in roads and vehicle traffic, are slowly closing off the elk's options."

Doug Houston, research biologist for Olympic National Park, agrees. "I'd say the major threat to the east-side elk is increased urbanization of winter range, especially along the river bottoms and riparian areas. These are the areas that appear to be critical during severe winter storms." Of course, no one can predict future weather patterns, but by using historic sources

♦

*Moth and rhododendron,
Duckabush River Valley,
Olympic National Forest*

Houston has estimated that episodes of "deep, dense, persistent snows" have affected the Peninsula's elk about six times over the past seventy to eighty years. "The east-side population is small by comparison," Houston explained, "and probably the most precarious. They're also quite different from elk on the west side of the park. They utilize different vegetation types, and have different adaptations and patterns of habitat use. As a major pre-serve for elk in the Northwest, the park needs to hang on to elk in all their forms in the Olympics."

I heard similar concerns talking to fisheries managers about the wild salmon and steelhead runs in east Olympic rivers. These concerns all point to a problem that, to some degree, affects all of Washington's remaining free-flowing streams. Rivers and their watersheds are integrated natural systems. In terms of their fisheries, their wildlife communities, and their forests, they function as single components within larger ecosystems. Yet nowhere are they managed as such. The Dosewallips and the rivers of the east Olympics are some of the most intact, functioning, whole watershed systems remaining in the Northwest. Numerous studies attest to their national significance as outstanding scenic, natural, and recreational resources. Yet they are classic examples of the kind of fragmentation and cumulative unraveling of a resource that results from multiple-agency management.

Scientists and conservationists have joined in calling for an "ecosystem approach" to the management of our national parks and wildlands. Such an approach would look beyond arbitrary administrative boundaries to ecological units like watersheds, taking the health of the whole interrelated life-community—trees, soils, streams, fish, wildlife, and people—into consideration. Needless to say, this would require the close cooperation of agencies and landowners, public and private, who haven't been overly cooperative in the past. But if we value the natural heritage of our parks and public resources, as well as the economic productivity of our industrial and private lands, such an approach is essential.

Designating the Dosewallips and other east Olympic streams as Wild and Scenic Rivers is a necessary first step. It would, at the very least, place a single agency in a monitoring role for the entire river resource. As with the Skagit Wild and Scenic River, that agency could then advise state, county, and local governments on management strategies that would protect the river's intrinsic, outstanding values. Without such oversight, we can only expect continued degradation of our river systems. The Dosewallips is a case in point.

A major hydroelectric development is proposed for the Dosewallips Valley

on Forest Service land immediately outside the national park boundary. The dam, intake structure, mile-long tunnel, penstock, powerhouse, transmission lines, and access roads would all be located on a steep, narrow corridor along the river between two nationally designated Wilderness areas. Impacts on downstream salmon and steelhead runs, and on migratory elk who pass through the area, are difficult to quantify, but numerous fishery, wildlife, and tribal agencies have expressed their concern. The project's developers, Jefferson County Public Utility District No. 1 and the city of Tacoma, have done little to reassure those concerned. The former is proceeding with utter disregard for a 63 percent majority of the county's voters who are opposed to such projects, and the latter's track record in its treatment of wild fish runs in other Northwest rivers is reprehensible.

The world scientific community has twice recognized Olympic National Park as a planetary resource. The United Nations Educational Scientific, and Cultural Organization has designated Olympic National Park as an International Biosphere Reserve, and a World Heritage site. In 1984 Congress included much of the undeveloped portion of the Dosewallips Valley in the National Wilderness System. That the Dosewallips is a river of national significance is beyond question.

◆

I sometimes think of that marten I encountered on the river trail as the embodiment of wilderness, a sign that the naturally evolved processes and intricately balanced systems are still in perfect working order. That's the promise the Olympic wilderness holds out, tenuously, for the future. That, and the mystery of those small mammalian eyes peering across from the other side of civilization to see just what it is we're all about.

"Scientists and conservationists have joined in calling for an 'ecosystem approach' to the management of our national parks and wildlands, taking the health of the whole interrelated life community—trees, soils, streams, fish, wildlife, and people—into consideration."

Snake

In 1834, Captain B. L. E. Bonneville led a small exploratory expedition down the spectacular canyons of the Snake River. Bonneville kept extensive records of his travels and these were eventually incorporated into Washington Irving's nineteenth-century classic *The Adventures of Captain Bonneville*. Quite popular in its time, it was through *The Adventures* that the American public was first introduced to the overpowering beauty of the Snake River canyon.

At times, the river was overhung by dark stupendous rocks, rising like gigantic walls and battlements; these would be rent by wide and yawning chasms that seemed to speak of past convulsions of nature. Sometimes the river was of a glassy smoothness and placidity, at other times it roared along in impetuous rapids and foaming cascades. Here, the rocks were piled in the most fantastic crags and precipices; and in another place they were succeeded by delightful valleys carpeted with greensward. The whole of this wide and varied scenery was dominated by immense mountains rearing their distant peaks into the clouds.

Irving, himself no stranger to the landscapes of the Far West, concluded the passage by venturing that "the Snake River must be one of the most remarkable for varied and striking scenery of all the rivers of this continent." A century and a half later, his observation still rings true.

Bonneville and his company were not the first whites to visit the Snake. In the fall of 1805, the Lewis and Clark expedition descended the Clearwater River to camp on the Snake across from what is now Clarkston, Washington. They then continued down the Snake, past the mouths of the Tucannon and Palouse rivers to their final juncture with the Columbia. By joining the Snake at Clarkston, Lewis and Clark avoided the tumultuous canyon country that would later make so strong an impression on Captain Bonneville. Not so the ill-fated Hunt party who followed "more or less" in Lewis and Clark's tracks six years later. They met the now-famous whitewater of Hells Canyon head on.

William Price Hunt was a gentleman, a man of "probity and worth" if we can accept Washington Irving's word, but whatever his acumen as a business representative for John Jacob Astor's Pacific Fur Company, one senses that wilderness survival was not one of his strong points. Hunt lead the overland portion of Astor's first expedition into the fur-trapping country west of the Rockies. The remainder of the expedition traveled on the ship

♦

Opposite: *Palouse Falls, near the confluence of the Snake River*
This page: *Yellow-bellied marmot*

♦

This page: *Yellow-bellied marmot*

Opposite: *Grande Ronde River near its confluence with the Snake River*

Tonquin around the Horn from New York. They were to reunite at the mouth of the Columbia River, where they would establish the trading post of Astoria.

Hunt's party did tolerably well at first, making the trip from St. Louis to the upper Snake River country in six months, but there his luck ended. In late fall, Hunt decided to assemble a fleet of canoes and "float" the rest of the way to the Columbia. It was a poor choice. They lost three of their fifteen boats the first day out, and things deteriorated from there. Unlike Captain Clark, Hunt frequently traveled without benefit of Indian guides or interpreters. Lacking good advice, the party continued down the Snake into even more serious water, and Hunt lost one of his best men. The destruction of several more boats reduced the party's stores to five days' provisions. In desperation, and with winter coming on, Hunt elected to split the party into smaller groups. The fate of these hapless, starving pilgrims is well documented in Irving's *Astoria*. What is remarkable is that one group of Hunt's voyagers actually did continue down the Snake River by boat. Somehow, they successfully navigated the treacherous cataracts of Hells Canyon to emerge alive (though slightly the worse for wear) where the canyon empties at the mouth of the Grande Ronde in what is now southeast Washington.

Hunt's men didn't name the rugged cataract Hells Canyon, though well they might have. To his French voyagers, it was *la maudite riviere enragée,* "the accursed mad river."

Today, some of the grandest reaches of the Snake River, where it flows through that "wide and varied scenery" that so impressed itself on Hunt's and Bonneville's men, have been permanently set aside as part of the Hells Canyon Natural Recreation Area.

Hells Canyon is bordered on the west by the Wallowa Mountains of Oregon and Washington, and on the east by the Seven Devils region of Idaho. Reaching a maximum depth of 7,900 feet, Hells Canyon is the deepest river-carved trench in North America, exceeding Arizona's Grand Canyon by more than a thousand feet. Within this steep, rock-walled terrain lies a wonderful diversity of wildlife, miles of hiking trails, exciting whitewater, and splendid scenery. It is also a land with its own timeless history. This stretch of the Snake has been inhabited by humans for eight thousand years, and the canyon bottom is still alive with the village sites, burial grounds, petroglyphs, and rock paintings of Indian cultures that long preceded our own.

And, of course, there is the river itself. Some seventy miles of it—as it knifes down along the rock cliffs and boulders from the Hells Canyon Dam almost to the Washington-Oregon line—are protected in the Recreation Area. The Snake flows unobstructed for an additional thirty miles beyond the Hells Canyon National Recreation Area, along Washington's southeast border, before it pools in the reservoir formed by the lower Granite Dam in the vicinity of Asotin, Washington. Along this, its last free stretch, the river jogs to the west to pick up the serpentine rush of the Grande Ronde—itself a splendid free-flowing river—then widens and gentles for the remainder of its unchecked journey north.

Of the Snake River's thousand-mile length from its source on the Yellowstone Plateau to its merger with the Columbia River at Pasco, this one hundred miles is its last major undammed reach.

The "accursed mad river" of Hunt's voyagers is a working river now. No fewer than fifteen dams have stilled most of its turbulent rush. Power, irrigation, and developed recreation are the primary uses of the Snake today. But as recently as the mid-1960s, it looked like those would be the river's only uses.

◆

*Phlox, Snake River
corridor*

A permit was issued then for construction of the High Mountain Sheep Dam in Hells Canyon, and it was only an eleventh-hour action by the United States Supreme Court that stopped its construction. In a momentous decision, William O. Douglas, writing for the Court, questioned the need to dam the last unchecked stretch of the Snake. He raised the issues of fish, wildlife, and recreation values, and the question of the greatest good to the public. The Court's decision sent the project back to the drawing boards, and this hiatus enabled conservationists to regroup for a final effort to save the canyon. This culminated in 1975 when Congress created the Hells Canyon National Recreation Area.

The National Recreation Area, however, extended north only to a point four miles above the Washington border. Congress directed that the remaining thirty-three miles of free-flowing river, nearly all along Washington's southeast border, be studied for inclusion in the National Wild and Scenic Rivers System. The study, released in 1985, recommended that this entire reach of the Snake be added to the system. Wild and Scenic status for this portion of the Snake, the study indicated, would complete the protection of Hells Canyon, which actually extends north to the mouth of the Grande Ronde, seven miles into Washington. It would also protect the twenty-two-mile downstream portion of the river that provides some of the last native spawning grounds for the Snake's runs of chinook salmon and summer steelhead. And it would keep for us, too, something of our past.

Less than two years after this study was released, however, an eastern power company filed with the Federal Energy Regulatory Commission for two dam sites on this part of the Snake. One was to be located just upstream from the town of Asotin, the other above the mouth of the Grande Ronde. Together they would have inundated the entire Asotin reach, backing water nearly to the boundary of the Hells Canyon Recreation Area at the Washington-Oregon line. As opposition to the projects began to mount, the Asotin County PUD took advantage of a recent law and filed "over" the eastern company's application for the lower dam site. Their reasoning, presumably, was that if anyone was going to destroy their river for profit, it would be them! The Federal Energy Regulatory Commission concurred, and in 1988 granted Asotin County a preliminary permit for exclusive use of the site.

At this point, opposition to any dam construction on this part of the river reached its peak, particularly on the more densely populated Idaho side of the river, and Congress began to take notice. Senator James McClure and Representative Larry Craig, both of Idaho, introduced a bill that prohibited dam construction on this portion of the Snake River. The measure passed late in 1988, and FERC was directed to issue no further permits for hydroelectric development, thus ensuring that the Asotin reach will remain free-flowing for the foreseeable future.

While conservationists and river users hailed this measure, they also made it clear that, in their view, this was an intermediate step. The law failed to address the questions of public access to the river corridor, and recreational management in general. Both needs had been outlined in the congressional study. Nor was mention made of livestock grazing levels along the river, a proposed limestone mining operation, and the proliferation of subdivisions along the rustic and natural river corridor. It was obvious that these and other issues would only be addressed in a comprehensive management plan resulting from the inclusion of this portion of the Snake in the National Wild and Scenic Rivers System. Clearly, the job is still undone.

The year 2005 will mark the bicentennial of Lewis and Clark's first glimpse of the Snake River's turbid waters. We have been more than successful in taming the "accursed mad river," and shaping it to our wants. Now, perhaps, it's time to grant the last of this wild, heroic river its license to be.

"William O. Douglas . . . questioned the need to dam the last unchecked stretch of the Snake. He raised the issues of fish, wildlife, and recreation values, and the question of the greatest good to the public."

Little Spokane

Mark Schulz and I lifted our paddles and let the canoe drift with the current. Before us, the rust brown shape of a marsh hawk sat motionless on a weathered post. Her cool, ember-red eyes held us intently as we passed a few paddle-lengths away. With field glasses I studied the fine, stippled shades of her plumage, the pale, snakelike skin of her feet. She was the third bird of prey we'd seen in less than an hour that morning. Just as I lowered the glasses, the long-legged form of a blue heron appeared on the opposite bank, its breast feathers ruffling in the breeze. Behind it, the raised "flag" of a white-tailed deer bounded off through stiff winter brush.

We had put in on the lower reach of eastern Washington's Little Spokane River that morning, nine miles above its confluence with the larger Spokane River. At this point the Little Spokane is a cold, clear stream that flows in wide meanders and sandy riffles through some of the richest wildlife habitat east of the Cascades. Almost immediately I began to notice ways in which this small, spring-fed stream differed from others I'd visited. One was its vegetation. The bulrushes, iris, and loosestrife that grew along the river's banks were marsh plants, common enough to sloughs and ponds, but rarely found along flowing streams. The wetlands and sedge meadows that bordered the river were more reminiscent of a coastal estuary than an inland gorge in the heart of eastern Washington's plateau country. And the sheer abundance of wildlife was dizzying.

Mark, on the other hand, seemed almost apologetic. "Actually," he conceded, "this is a slow time of year for birds. The summer residents have already left, and the winter birds are just starting to arrive. But it *is* hard to believe we're less than two miles from Spokane's city limits, isn't it?" He smiled from the stern of the canoe and continued. "I guess that's another thing that makes this such a unique stretch of river. It's virtually surrounded by roads, housing developments, and high arid plateau lands, but it's still one of the most productive year-round habitats in the state."

For the past several years Mark has worked as a ranger at nearby Riverside State Park. Part of his duties include management of the newly designated Little Spokane River Natural Area. Mark admits that's what attracted him to the job, and it's the part of his work he enjoys most. As we drifted down the slow meanders past mergansers and pintails, I had to confess that I could think of a few worse jobs.

◆

Opposite: *Yellow irises, Little Spokane River*
This page: *Great blue heron*

". . . one of our big challenges as managers is to make sure that human use and 'appreciation' of this area don't actually destroy the very things people are coming to see."

The river flows westerly, and steep, rocky bluffs rise to the north and south. These isolate and protect the river bottom to a degree, and help create the ideal breeding and nesting conditions that attract more than one hundred thirty bird species here each year. Even in the chill and overcast of the late fall morning, the lushness of the river's wetlands formed a marked contrast to the arid, rocky pine bluffs to the north. "It's that variety of habitats," Mark said, "the mix of grassy pine slopes, marsh grass wetlands, pasture, river, and those dense fir forests of the southern slopes that accommodates such a diversity of species. And all within a relatively short and narrow corridor." As Mark spoke he angled his paddle and swung the bow of the canoe toward a side channel.

I'd noticed several channels in various stages of "abandonment" by the river as it shifted its course and built sandbars across their entrances. We ducked beneath some overhanging brush at the entrance and used our paddles to "pole" across the bar. Once through, a quiet, almost pondlike channel opened before us. A flock of wood ducks paddled off around a bend, and a heron rose noisily from the reeds. Mark pointed out thick beds of pondweed growing just beneath the channel's surface.

"This stuff harbors all kinds of little crustaceans that are an important food for those wood ducks," he said. "Painted turtles, too. In summer you can see driftwood logs covered with painted turtles, all of them just hanging out in the sun. It's a colorful sight. And those mud flats along the inside bends are full of worms and bugs for sandpipers, killdeers, and snipe." A killdeer or two were, in fact, darting among the bank weeds. "These slow-water channels are also nurseries for fish, which makes excellent hunting for herons, mergansers, muskrats. . . ." he laughed. "The list goes on."

I could tell Mark was reluctant to leave the channel, but the river went on, too, and my cold hands were having trouble keeping up my notes. He didn't have to worry about that; he was wearing mittens. Finally we popped out onto the river a surprisingly short distance from where we had ducked in. "Oh yeah," Mark said with a laugh, "that's another thing broad meanders do: they *create habitat!*"

The river carried us past forested slopes where the song of a nuthatch filtered down through the trees, and past a beaver colony where smaller trees were girdled or felled and their branches stripped bare for food. Though we listened for the warning "thwack!" of a beaver tail slapping the surface, it didn't come. "Maybe they don't think we're a threat," I offered. Nevertheless, none of them saw fit to make an appearance. We passed an old farmhouse or two, and a snag by a bridge that a pileated woodpecker called home. Winter birds worked the brush for rose hips and snowberries, and schools of large sleepy fish that looked like carp lay low in shimmering green pools.

By the time we came to the heron rookery near the end of our float, I'd given up on recording sightings and put on a pair of thick wool gloves. The river straightened, after a bend, and a corridor opened up on a steep, notched cliff face rising abruptly to the north. A tall stand of cottonwoods marked one side of the corridor, and high in the crooks of limbs I could see the large, ungainly stick nests where great blue herons had raised their young in spring and summer. By now the herons, or most of them, had left for the open waters of warmer climes, and the bare branches and empty nests swayed in the wind. Mark said that this past year twenty active nests were counted in the rookery, down from a high of thirty some years earlier. "That may be simply natural fluctuation," he explained, "but one of our big challenges as managers is to make sure that human use and 'appreciation' of this area don't actually destroy the very things people are coming to see. That's why our management plan has placed restrictions on activities like camping, swimming, inner-tubing . . . things people are used to doing in state parks. Instead we encourage passive, low-density uses like hiking, canoeing, cross-country skiing, and nature study, things that are more in keeping with a 'natural area' designation. It's a delicate balance."

Delicate may be too mild a term, particularly when one considers that not too many years ago, most of this area was privately owned and slated for development. I wondered how it was that this little jewel of a valley ultimately came to be acquired and permanently set aside for wildlife and "light impact" recreation. "For that perspective, you'll have to talk to someone who's been around here a bit longer than I have," Mark deferred. "You might try Morey Haggin."

◆

It's difficult to separate Morey Haggin from the river he's worked tirelessly to preserve. His clear, hazel eyes glint beneath white, bushy brows when he talks of the Little Spokane, and his voice lilts and falls with the cadence of a rippling stream. After living on the Little Spokane River for fifty-four of his eighty-two years, Morey's is as sure and strong a voice as any wild river could have on its behalf. And for the Little Spokane, that voice couldn't have arrived at a better time.

A day after canoeing the Little Spokane, I spoke with Morey Haggin about his life on the river, and the efforts he and others made to have part of it preserved. Morey leaned back in his chair, folded his hands at his chin, and smiled. "Well, I suppose we should go back to the beginning, shouldn't we."

The beginning, in this instance, was the thirties. The Depression lay like a heavy cloud over the Pacific Northwest when Morey found his way here from Osage Indian country in Oklahoma. If it was good fortune that landed him a job with Great Northern Railroad, it was extreme good fortune that enabled him and his wife, Margaret, to raise

◆

Redwing blackbird and wild roses, Little Spokane River Natural Area

◆

the thousand dollars needed to buy seventeen acres of choice riverfront land on the Little Spokane River when it came up for sale. "I was a great fly fisherman in those days," Morey told me. "The Little Spokane was the closest trout stream around, and I'd come out to the river often. I'd fished most of the river by that time—of course, it was all privately owned and posted," he chuckled. "I'd get kicked out of it regularly."

It was on these trips that the Haggins first became enchanted with the river and its lush corridor. It was also then that they noted the area's richness as wildlife habitat. "Oh, we'd sight deer, beaver, weasels, muskrat, raccoons, mink, an occasional coyote, and a wonderful host of resident and migratory birds." Morey remembers the year he and Margaret recorded 168 bird species on their property alone, "and that's just what we happened to see around the place. I think the area may have over two hundred species, so it's

pretty productive by anybody's standards." Since then, Morey and Margaret have taken part in many of the Audubon Society's Christmas bird counts. He remembers one Christmas when forty species were recorded along the stream. "And that was in temperatures ranging to twenty below. And snowing!"

The Haggins realized that this kind of abundance was remarkable, particularly for an area a mere half-dozen miles from the bustle of downtown Spokane. "We saw that it was an area that deserved protection, so we began to explore how that might be done." Working with area conservation groups, together with concerned sportsmen and property owners, Morey and Margaret sought protection for the lower, undeveloped portion of the Little Spokane River and its associated marshes and wetlands. Since the entire river was privately owned, this was a difficult prospect. By the late sixties, Morey's persistence led him to the door of the newly appointed director of the Spokane County Parks Department, Sam Angove.

"When Morey Haggin first approached me about the Little Spokane," Angove told me, "I'd just arrived here from northern California where the long campaign for Redwood National Park had recently been resolved." After visiting the river with Morey and others, Angove was convinced. And his experience in the redwood country had impressed upon him the need to act quickly. With the help of available federal and state funding, and generous contributions of private lands, Angove and the county began building a preserve along the lower river the hard way. They bought it, parcel by parcel.

Broad-based support, good timing, and the dedicated efforts of many local citizens enabled Spokane County to secure nearly eight hundred acres of pristine habitat. Then, in the early eighties, the federal purse strings drew shut. "That's when the state legislature took an active part in acquiring an additional six hundred acres along the river as state park lands," Angove explained, "but it was never Morey Haggin's or anyone's idea that the area be developed into a high-use recreational park facility." So special legislation was developed, and introduced in the state capitol at Olympia, to create the Little Spokane River Natural Area. The preserve would be jointly owned by the county and the state, and

managed by the Washington State Parks and Recreation Commission under the kinds of "passive and low-density" directives Mark Schulz had described to me on the river the previous day. A premium would be placed on environmental education, and an interpretive center is planned for the site. But human enjoyment of the area would be contingent on preserving the outstanding natural values that first drew Morey Haggin to the river more than a half century before.

This kind of management was fairly new and untried ground for state park managers, but given the ever-increasing demands placed on existing recreation areas, Mark Schulz sees it as the kind of challenge park managers may soon have to face in other parts of the state as well.

Toward the end of our canoe trip on the river, I had asked Mark how he thought the Little Spokane Natural Area fit into the larger picture of wildlife conservation in the Northwest. He thought for a moment before answering. "What's been saved on the Little Spokane is just one small vestige of a vanishing America," he told me. "This little area won't save a species, or even a population, but it's one small piece of the puzzle that gives some hope for the future." I remember thinking that day, even as winter closed down over the bare trees and pine bluffs of the Little Spokane Valley, that from the bow of a canoe on that slow, meandering stream, the future looked darned good.

"What's been saved on the Little Spokane is just one small vestige of a vanishing America. . . it's one small piece of the puzzle that gives some hope for the future."

Kettle

Maybe it was the lateness of the season: that fresh dusting of snow on Sherman Creek Pass. Maybe it was the weeks on the road crisscrossing the state with notebook, thermos, and maps. Whatever the reason, I was growing a little weary of travel, and my thoughts were beginning to turn toward home. But my interest had recently been piqued by a certain highland river that meandered snakelike back and forth across the Canadian border to the north. The Kettle River watershed heads in British Columbia's Monashee Mountains and sprawls across portions of two sovereign nations, two counties, and manages to nip at a couple of national forests along the way. Behavior like this brings to mind the words of a river study published a few years ago. It stated in its introduction that rivers flow downhill "with blatant disregard for jurisdictional boundaries." The Kettle, however, along with the Skagit and Columbia rivers in Washington, one-upped the study by raising the ante from administrative boundaries to national ones. A very riverlike thing to do, I thought, adding a touch of humility to our notions of nationalism and self-importance.

I also recalled a conversation I had had with Morey Haggin. We were talking about fly-fishing on the Little Spokane River when Morey broadened the discussion to include most of the eastern part of the state. "If eastern Washington has anything that could be considered a blue-ribbon trout stream," he told me, "it's the Kettle River." He went on to talk about the quality of the Kettle's waters, its fine spawning gravels and lovely setting, then he added, "As far as trout waters go, the Kettle is probably as close as we Washingtonians will ever come to streams like the Madison or Yellowstone." I had long since learned that excellent trout streams must also be prime producers of insects, bacteria, and algae; they must be clean-flowing with shaded leafy banks, and they must, of necessity, be excellent habitat for wildlife: eagles, osprey, waterfowl, otters, mink, and voles. Also, having spent some time a few summers earlier in that stunning northern Rockies country, I thought I'd best put one more jog in my journey home and have a look.

Curlew, Washington, is a wisp of a town. It lies tucked along the Kettle River amidst the rolling hill country of northeast Washington, fairly well off just about anyone's beaten path. But if autumn had scattered itself tastefully around the Northwest's mountain valleys that year, it lavished itself on the Kettle River above

♦

Opposite: *Autumn leaves in the Kettle River*
This page: *Wild rose*

◆

Opposite: *Fall on the Kettle River above Curlew*

Curlew. All along its length, as the river ribboned through its narrow valley, the rustling, gold-green crowns of cottonwood trees highlighted the banks like a muted torchlight procession.

It was late afternoon by the time I turned up-valley along the East Kettle River Road. Small farms and cut pastures spread along bottomlands between the hill slopes and river. Bluffs to the south were covered with sparse stands of forest; to the north they stepped down in shallow cliffs and smooth, benchlike terraces of grassland and pine. A bright splash of crimson sumac fringed an occasional rock slope, and pale yellow aspens shivered lightly in the breeze. The gray rock and dust-dry grasses of the valley slopes formed a striking contrast with the green irrigated pastures along the river. Weather-browned barns stacked with hay bales stood at the edges of fenced fields, and clusters of cows and horses grazed silently in the autumn light.

Unlike the more mountainous rivers of the Cascades and Olympics, the Kettle is a pastoral river, bordering the edges of farmlands and woodlots, and its banks are almost entirely privately owned. It was to protect rivers such as the Kettle, where federal Wild and Scenic management would seem inappropriate, that the state of Washington developed its State Scenic Rivers System. State protection for rivers is not as strong as federal protection, but it does give legal protection to streams included in the system. Local residents and river users work with state agencies to develop a management plan for the river. The Federal Energy Regulatory Commission gives special status to state-protected rivers as well. In addition, efforts are coordinated among all state agencies so that projects such as highway and bridge reconstruction or recreational developments are carried out in a manner that will least affect the scenic and recreational qualities of the stream. The state may also purchase scenic easements or recreational

"Poets, sages, and philosophers have found in the flow of the river—from its distant mountain headwaters to its ultimate union with the sea—a metaphor for life, and an image for the mystical journey of the spirit."

access from willing sellers along the river—something Morey Haggin and other fishermen have pointed out as being badly needed on the Kettle.

It didn't take me long, however, to leave the car and clamber down to the river where it cut close to the road. It was good to be outside again, and the air smelled of dampness and fall leaves. Cottonwoods along the far bank were ripening from soft peach to pumpkin, and their Monet-like reflections were lucent in the dark water. The river moved slowly against its banks, with a sound both deep and musical. There were no rapids or falls to break the river's mood. The upper Kettle is the kind of river that lures you to its banks to listen. I stopped where a small pile of sunken cottonwood leaves shimmered in an eddy, each leaf placed as if by a human hand. Other leaves floated by like tiny boats. They brought to mind the old Chinese poets who would brush their poems onto fine paper and set them to drift on the autumn waters of long ago.

◆

From the earliest beginnings of what we know as civilization, when the first agricultural centers grew up around the fertile river valleys of Eurasia, rivers have been the focal points of life. Poets, sages, and philosophers have found in the flow of the river—from its distant mountain headwaters to its ultimate union with the sea—a metaphor for life, and an image for the mystical journey of the spirit. Throughout time, the river has been seen as immutable. Rains continue to fall, waters press on in their journey seaward, and ocean clouds rise and fall back against the timbered hills. The cycle ever renews itself in a process of seasonal change. Mountains lift and sift away, but the river remains.

"If there is magic on this planet, it is contained in water," wrote Loren Eiseley in *The Flow of the River*. ". . .It touches the past and prepares the future; it moves under the poles and wanders thinly in the heights of air. It can assume forms of exquisite perfection in a snowflake, or strip the living to a single shining bone cast up by the sea." Perhaps more than any other writer, Eiseley has evoked that long journey of humankind, from the "timeless ferment" of water, salt, and sunlight, to a mind that can conceive the *Brandenburg Concertos,* or savor the beauty of an autumn stream. Eiseley's words and the words of others came to mind as I sat by the Kettle that late afternoon. It's a river particularly well suited to riparian philosophy, and after a time I closed my notebook and let the current carry my thoughts where it would. Such musings, I know, are difficult to catalog when weighing the "values" of rivers. They can't be parceled out into megawatts or measured in cubic feet per second. And they don't really lend themselves well to being sorted out into "visitor days," though I confess to lingering in this exquisite valley, "inviting my soul" as Whitman liked to say.

Something curious happens to me around flowing water. It's been this way ever since I was a child. Thoughts about having to get back home have a way of, well, slipping off. And though I no longer come dragging in late for dinner with muddy sneakers and soaked jeans, I sometimes find that, once around rivers and streams, I rearrange my priorities by default. It's not that I forget about going home, just that "going home" seems to lose its relevance.

It's this, I think, that each of us recognizes in the eddy and flow of running water. That this watery earth, adrift in the cold and dusty immensities of space, is the only real home we know. We hear it in the musical clatter of rivers as they sweep and braid across the tilting continents. And the coursing in our veins knows it to be true.

Afternoon faded toward evening as I meandered along the riverbank. The reflected colors darkened and there

◆

This page: *Riverside home, Kettle River*

Overleaf: *Marsh marigolds and moss, Cle Elum River*
Inset: *Great spangled fritillary*

was a faint taste of snow in the air. A rumble caused me to look up and see an older man cantering his horse across a bridge, a small hound panting close behind. The clip-clop of hooves echoed downstream with a familiar resonance. It could have been a century ago. A few cows lowed softly in a distant pasture, and the ring of a splitting maul carried on the evening wind.

The Kettle River lingered in the late golden glow of the cottonwoods, then disappeared in a bend as the trees closed around it. Somewhere that night there would be moonlight scattering copper over this gently rippling water. Somewhere, someone would drift off to sleep listening to its song.

Part 3

by Douglass A. North

River Protection Programs

Both Washington State and the United States have programs available for the conservation of important natural rivers: the Washington Scenic Rivers Program and the National Wild and Scenic Rivers System. The two programs are very different in the protections that they provide, but they complement each other by addressing different conservation and management problems. Furthermore, management of lands along the rivers in the national program is quite different depending upon whether the river is added to the national system by Congress or transferred into the national system from the Washington State Scenic Rivers Program.

The basic philosophy of the Washington State Scenic Rivers Program is one of cooperative management of the river by local landowners, interested recreational users, and the state and local governments. The program does not have the power of eminent domain and does not impose any additional regulations on private land. It is best suited to dealing with problems of conflicts between landowners and recreational users, obtaining river access sites, providing sanitation and litter-disposal facilities, and getting local governments to cooperate in the conservation of the river.

The basic philosophy of the National Wild and Scenic Rivers System is to keep the river the way it is. The emphasis is on providing direction to the federal agencies responsible for determining much of the resource extraction and development that occurs along our most pristine rivers. Wild and Scenic designation provides direction to the Federal Energy Regulatory Commission (FERC) on dam licensing, to the USDA Forest Service on timber practices and road building, and to the Bureau of Land Management (BLM) on mining. It allows all existing development to continue, but discourages new development right on the riverbank where it would interfere with the natural values of the river.

On national rivers designated by Congress, limitations on development are accomplished by purchases of land or easements by the managing agency (the federal agency—usually the one with the most land along the river—given management authority on the designated river). On rivers transferred into the national system from the state system, the federal government has no authority to acquire land, and the river is managed like a river in the Washington State Scenic Rivers Program.

The Washington State Scenic Rivers Program

The Washington Scenic Rivers Program implements cooperative management by establishing a river council for each river added to the program. Each river council consists of a representative from each county through which the river flows, a representative from each incorporated town bordering the river, and the members of the Committee of Participating Agencies, which oversees the scenic river program. The Committee of Participating Agencies consists of two members of the public appointed by the governor and representatives from several state departments, including Ecology, Fisheries, Wildlife, Natural Resources, and Transportation. In addition, an advisory committee consisting of local landowners and recreational users is usually formed to advise and assist the river council.

What the State Program Does

Each river council is charged with developing a management plan for publicly owned or leased property along the river under its jurisdiction. The plan usually identifies whatever concerns local governments, landowners, and recreational users may have about the river and lists potential solutions to the problems identified. Common concerns include river access, trespass by recreational users, sanitation, and litter control.

The river council is charged with establishing the boundaries of the scenic river corridor within two years of its designation. The river council should base the width of the corridor on the amount of land along the river that must be involved in dealing with the problems identified. The corridor could be only 200 feet on each side of the high water mark (as it is on the Skykomish), or it could be much broader, perhaps a quarter mile on each side of the river. Prior to determining the boundaries, each river council is required to hold at least one public hearing near the river and will usually hold several.

The management plans developed by the river councils are administered by the State Parks and Recreation Department, which is required to coordinate the activities of all state agencies with regard to the rivers. The department is authorized to purchase land or easements in the river area to protect the scenic integrity of the corridor, fish and wildlife habitat, historical sites, camping and picnicking areas, boat-launching sites, and fishing-access sites.

All state agencies and local governments are directed to pursue policies in connection with their regular functions that will conserve and enhance rivers included in the program. At the national level, the Federal Energy Regulatory Commission (FERC), which licenses most hydroelectric projects, is required by federal law to consider the fact that the river has been designated as a state scenic river before it issues a license for a project on the river. The special recognition given to state scenic rivers should encourage local governments and local landowners to take particular pride in their rivers and work to keep them among the finest natural rivers in the state.

What the State Program Does Not Do

The Washington State Scenic Rivers Program does not impose any additional regulations on private land. It also does not give the government any power to force private landowners to sell any part of their land. Private landowners are free to ignore the program, and the State Parks and Recreation Department cannot make them do otherwise.

The program also does not prevent the departments of Fisheries or Wildlife from making "improvements" to scenic rivers in order to facilitate the passage or propagation of fish. In fact, state scenic-river designation has no effect whatsoever on fishing or hunting regulations. Nor does the program absolutely stop dams. Federal law allows FERC to license a dam on a state scenic river if it determines that the national interest in the development of power overrides the state interest in protecting the scenic river. In addition, the Army Corps of Engineers and the Bureau of Reclamation, the two agencies that have built most large federal dams, are free to ignore the state scenic designation.

Finally, the Washington State Scenic Rivers Program cannot direct the management of Forest Service or BLM lands along designated rivers. Generally, the federal agencies are very cooperative with the state government, but they do not have to take any direction from the state.

The National Wild And Scenic Rivers System

Under the National Wild and Scenic Rivers Act of 1968, a river is eligible to be designated Wild and Scenic if it is free-flowing and has one or more "outstandingly remarkable values," which can include scenery, recreation, fish and wildlife, geology, history, culture, or ecology. Dams or other water projects that would seriously interfere with these values may not be built on or along National Wild and Scenic Rivers. This resulting protection represents the most significant effect of National Wild and Scenic Rivers designation. In short, it stops FERC, the Army Corps of Engineers, the Bureau of Reclamation, individual states, and everyone else from destroying the free-flowing nature of designated rivers.

The management of lands along designated rivers depends, in large measure, on whether the river was added to the system by Congress or transferred to the system at the request of individual states.

CONGRESSIONALLY DESIGNATED RIVERS

Most rivers are added to the National Wild and Scenic Rivers System by acts of Congress following studies to determine whether they are eligible to be part of the system and what special values each one has that should be managed for protection. Such studies are done by federal agencies (such as the USDA Forest Service, National Park Service, or Bureau of Land Management) pursuant to direction from Congress or as part of their regular land-management-planning process

In the plans that the Forest Service drew up for the national forests in Washington in the 1980s, it reviewed over 100 rivers flowing through the national forests to determine which should be designated as Wild and Scenic rivers. The plans are not final as of this writing, but it is expected that the agency will find between 70 and 80 Washington rivers to be eligible and will recommend to Congress that between 30 and 40 of those be designated as Wild and Scenic.

What Congressional Designation Does

Designation of a river results in its classification as wild, scenic, or recreational and in the development of a management plan for it. The management plan gives specific direction to the federal agencies on how they are to treat the river and the lands along its banks.

Classification

Each section of a congressionally designated river is to be classified as "wild, scenic or recreational." These names are somewhat misleading because they have nothing to do with the scenery along the river or how much recreation it provides. Instead, they refer to the relative amount of human development that exists along the river at the time of its designation. Each river can have several different sections with different classifications.

A "wild" river section is one in nearly natural condition. It cannot have any roads paralleling it and can generally be reached only by trail or boat. It cannot have any evidence of timber harvest or farm fields, but it can have some livestock grazing. There are few sections of river in Washington, outside of already designated national parks and wilderness areas, that qualify as wild.

A "scenic" river section is one that is still largely natural, but has some evidence of human development. It can be paralleled by a road, provided that the road is generally not visible from the river. It can have occasional bridges across it, and scattered cabins and homes along it, as well as agricultural land and commercial forests.

A "recreational" river section can have almost any amount of development along it as long as the river still has at least one outstanding natural value. For example, a recreational river can have a highway or railroad right along its bank, can be crossed by numerous bridges, or can flow through towns.

Whichever classification is applied, it represents both a description of a river's condition at the time of designation and a goal for managing the river. For example, the managing agency should not allow new roads to be built into a wild river corridor and should not allow real estate subdivision in a scenic river corridor.

Management Plans

Besides halting dams and adverse water projects, designation of a river as wild, scenic, or recreational requires that the managing agency develop a plan to manage, protect, and enhance the natural values of the river. The plan should include specific direction to federal agencies on the siting of roads, campgrounds, power lines, mines, water projects, and the lay-out of timber sales on government-owned lands. The responsibility for seeing that these directions are carried out rests with the managing agency specified by Congress in the Act designating the river. The managing agency is generally the federal agency that has the most land along the designated portion of the river, but state and local governments or Indian tribes can be partners with a federal agency in managing the river. (Note: Because the managing agency in Washington state is usually the Forest Service, it is assumed to be so in the rest of this discussion.)

The first step in developing a plan to protect the river is to determine the boundaries of its river corridor. The Forest Service is required to make this determination within a year after the river is designated. It must seek public input on the boundary determination by holding a series of public meetings, developing a set of proposed boundaries, getting comments from the public, and then developing a set of final boundaries based upon the public comment. The boundaries are normally about one-quarter mile on each side of the river, but they can be set narrower in some places and wider in others. The boundaries are to be drawn to protect the special values that Congress designated the river to protect. Therefore, the boundaries could be, say, a mile wide to take in a wetland next to the river or only 100 yards wide where a highway runs next to the river.

After determining the boundaries, the Forest Service works on the management plan. First, the agency holds meetings to determine which issues and problems members of the public think the plan should address. (Should the plan address river access, potential mining, protection of elk and deer winter range, sanitation problems, or what?) After getting public input and doing its own research, the Service develops a draft plan, which it prints and makes available to the public. The agency then holds a second series of meetings, in which the public is invited to comment on the draft plan. Interested parties also submit written commentary on the draft. The Forest Service then makes changes in the draft based upon the comments and publishes a final plan. Anyone dissatisfied with the final plan can appeal it.

The Forest Service's Forest Planning Handbook already contains guidelines for managing national forest land along Wild and Scenic rivers. These guidelines, which apply only to federal land, constitute a generic plan of sorts that then can be adapted to individual rivers (see Appendix for a copy of the guidelines).

What Congressional Designation Does Not Do

Wild and Scenic designation does a lot less than many people think. It strikes a compromise between protecting natural values and private property rights. In fact, it has more protections for private property owners than any other major piece of federal natural resources legislation.

Effects on Adjacent Land

Wild and Scenic designation has no direct effect on private property. After designation, private landowners can do anything they want with their land. To stop a landowner from using property in a way that would harm the natural values of the river, the Forest Service would have to buy the land or an interest in it. (The service can buy an interest in the land by purchasing an easement to restrict development while leaving ownership of the land with the landowner.)

The Forest Service, however, does have the power of eminent domain, which means that it can force a landowner to sell. But the Wild and Scenic Rivers Act specifically says that the agency cannot force a landowner to sell outright if more than 50 percent of the land along the river already belongs to federal, state, or local governments. (That is, it cannot force the owner to sell all of the land. It can only purchase an interest in the land that would restrict further development.) This is true of all of the rivers proposed for designation in Washington except for a few river sections that no one lives along on the South Fork and Middle Fork Nooksack, the Palouse, and the Klickitat rivers.

Where the government already owns more than half of the land along a river, the only means the Forest Service has to control development that would hurt the river is to buy scenic easements. When it does so, the Service, in effect, buys the development rights to the land. Landowners can continue to use the land just as they had before, or rent it, sell it, or leave it to their children, but they can't develop it. Generally, scenic easements are windfalls to riverside landowners, who are paid well for the easement and find that their property is worth more than it was before, because people will pay a premium for land along a protected river.

Designation also has no effect on existing water rights. Water rights applied for after designation, however, may be limited to make sure that enough water remains in the river to support the natural values for which the river was designated.

Effects on Resource Development

Wild and Scenic designation does not halt timber harvesting, mining, and other resource development on federal lands along a river, though it places limitations on these activities to make sure they do not adversely affect the river. The limitations can take effect on private property only if the Forest Service buys an interest in the property, since designation has no direct effect on private property.

On Forest Service and BLM lands, new mining claims cannot be filed in wild-river corridors, but already existing claims can still be worked. New claims can be made within scenic- and recreational-river corridors, but such claims are subject to conditions set by the managing agency to see that they do not harm water quality and do not infringe on the natural values for which the river was designated.

Timber harvesting practices on publicly owned land remain largely unaffected along "recreational" river segments. The managing agency must insure that harvest does not harm the outstandingly remarkable values that caused the river to be designated. In other words, the Forest Service and BLM must apply their normal standards for protecting riparian and wildlife areas and other outstanding natural values and must not cut right on the bank of the river. Along Scenic and Wild segments, however, stricter provisions apply. First, no timber harvesting is allowed on the few sections of river that qualify as wild. Second, along scenic sections, harvesting must be back from the bank and consist only of selective logging and small clearcuts; there can be no large clearcuts within a one-quarter mile of the river.

STATE-TRANSFERRED RIVERS

A river protected by the Washington State Scenic Rivers Program can be transferred into the national Wild and Scenic Rivers System if the governor asks the secretary of the interior to do so. Upon receiving such a request, the secretary's staff studies the river to determine its eligibility for inclusion in the national system. If the nominated river qualifies, it can be transferred to the national system at the secretary's discretion. The secretary, however, is under no obligation to agree to the governor's request.

What State Transfer Does

Transfer of a state scenic river into the national system gives the river the special protections of the national system, particularly the absolute ban on dams and harmful water projects. It also directs the Forest Service and BLM to manage resource development on adjacent public land just as it does along rivers designated by Congress.

The management of a state-transferred river, however, rests with the state; the Wild and Scenic Rivers Act specifically says that such a river is to be managed at no cost to the federal government. The State Parks and Recreation Department continues to implement whatever management plan it drew up when the river was first added to the state program. Implementation of the management plan is directed by the River Council.

What State Transfer Does Not Do

Transfer of a state scenic river into the federal system does not allow the federal government to acquire any land along the river. The Wild and Scenic Rivers Act only gives a federal agency land acquisition authority when the river is designated by Congress.

No land or any interest in land can be condemned along a state river that has been transferred into the federal system because (1) the federal government has no acquisition authority over such rivers and (2) state regulations governing administration of the river specify that condemnation cannot be used. As a result of these two restrictions, there is no way to prevent an owner of land along a state-transferred river from doing something that may harm the natural values of the river. With the necessary county permits, a landowner could build, say, condominiums, a casino, or a steel mill along the river.

Transfer of a state-protected river into the national system also has no impact on existing water rights. The Wild and Scenic Rivers Act explicitly leaves existing water rights intact, and the state lacks authority to acquire them.

Protection For Our Imperiled Rivers: Proposed Legislation

Washington's remaining wild rivers are imperiled by our failure to recognize and protect their natural values. Only a handful of our rivers are part of the state and federal river programs. For the rest, there is no coherent management, and their values are becoming more and more compromised. Dams impound sections, logging silts the water, mines poison the banks, and development destroys the scenery and habitat. On undesignated rivers, no agency is responsible for the overall health of the whole river. Only designation as a state or federally pro tected river will result in the management of the river as a whole.

To meet the challenge of preserving some of our wild river heritage, legislation has been proposed by conservationists at both the state and federal levels. The 1989 session of the Washington legislature saw a bill introduced to begin expansion of the state scenic rivers program by adding six rivers to the program (Green, Carbon, Cispus, Lewis, Washougal, and Little Spokane). The bill passed the House and the Senate Environment and Natural Resources Committee, but died in the Senate Rules Committee in a logjam over budget issues. It will be revived for 1990, perhaps with some additional rivers.

Federal Wild and Scenic designation is particularly needed because so many of our finest rivers flow through our national forests. A coalition of environmental groups has formed the Wild and Scenic Rivers Steering Committee to work jointly toward the passage of a good Wild and Scenic Rivers bill for Washington State. With representatives of the Northwest Rivers Council, Sierra Club, American Rivers, Washington Wilderness Coalition, Mountaineers, Olympic Rivers Council, Audubon and Wenatchee Rivers Conservation Coalition, among others, the committee will make a proposal on a Wild and Scenic bill to the Washington congressional delegation.

As of Fall 1989, the champions of river protection in the Washington delegation are Senator Brock Adams and Representative John Miller. The other members of the delegation have indicated a willingness to take part in a legislative process to determine which of Washington's rivers deserve Wild and Scenic protection, but have not made any commitment to extensive river protection. It is hoped that legislation will be introduced in early 1990 and that hearings on the bill will occur soon thereafter.

You can help protect Washington's rivers by expressing your views to your representative and our two senators. You can write to: Senator Brock Adams or Senator Slade Gorton, Senate Office Building, Washington, D.C. 20510; Representative John Miller, Representative Jolene Unsoeld, Representative Tom Foley, Representative Jim McDermott, Representative Al Swift, Representative Sid Morrison, Representative Norm Dicks, Representative Rod Chandler, House Office Building, Washington, D.C. 20515.

Washington's Wild Rivers: An Action List

The following is a list of Washington rivers deserving protection in the state or federal river protection programs. The list was compiled by the Northwest Rivers Council in consultation with other conservation groups, but it is not a final proposal, nor has it been endorsed by any organization. The list should be useful to a reader who would like to know about the special values of particular rivers and the threats to those rivers. Although the list of some 2,200 miles of rivers and creeks is less than 8 percent of Washington's named streams, it illustrates the enormous richness and diversity of Washington's finest flowing water.

The rivers on this list are those that have been found to have the most outstanding features or combination of features in Washington. These features have been documented in a number of studies of Washington rivers:

■ In 1980 and 1982 the National Park Service prepared the "Nationwide Rivers Inventory" of rivers that appeared to be eligible to become federal Wild and Scenic rivers.

■ In 1985-1986, the Bonneville Power Administration and Washington State conducted the Washington portion of the Northwest Rivers Study for the Northwest Power Planning Council. This study documented the relative value of each section of river for fish, wildlife, recreation, historical and cultural values and natural features.

■From 1986 through 1988, the seven national forests in Washington released draft plans on managing the forests. Each of the plans contains a section on the eligibility and classification of rivers in the forests that were considered as possible Wild and Scenic rivers.

In 1988, the Washington Parks and Recreation Commission issued a report finding 56 Washington rivers potentially eligible for the state scenic river program and recommending 18 rivers, upon which studies had been completed, for addition to the system.

For each river on this list, the larger body of water into which it flows is listed to help in locating the stream. Next, the Outstandingly Remarkable Values, which make it eligible for state or federal designation, are listed. Then, the threats to the river's natural condition are mentioned.

Segments and Classification indicate whether the river deserves state or federal designation or both, and the proper classification level for each section of the river under the federal Wild and Scenic Act. State Scenic River means that the river deserves state desgnation. Wild, Scenic, and Recreational indicate that the river deserves federal designation and the level of classification that is appropriate for that particular part of the river.

Some rivers have both federal classification listings and a state scenic river listing, indicating that the river deserves inclusion in both the state and federal programs.

The segments are generally divided at natural landmarks such as the mouth of a tributary creek or a road crossing. In some cases, however, it was necessary to divide segments at places where such a feature was not available. In those cases, the division has been made using the section, range, and township method of locating land. Each township is six miles long and six miles wide and is divided into 36 one-mile-square sections. The township listings run north and south and are given numbers so that Township 13 North can be abbreviated as T 13 N. The townships are cross-referenced with range numbers, which run east and west so that Range 36 East becomes R 36 E. The national forest maps show the township and range numbers in the margins, and the section numbers are printed on the maps. This allows for the location of any section by listing its township, range, and section number.

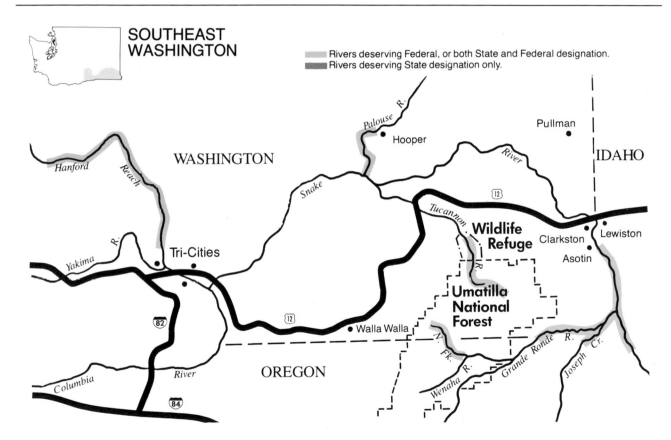

SOUTHEAST WASHINGTON

Rivers deserving Federal, or both State and Federal designation.
Rivers deserving State designation only.

■ GRANDE RONDE RIVER

Tributary of: Snake River
Outstandingly Remarkable Values: Fish, wildlife, recreation, scenery, ecology, history, culture
Threats: Hydroelectric dams, unmanaged recreational use
Segments & Classification
  Recreation: 11 miles (Oregon border to Buford Creek)
  Wild: 21.1 miles (Buford Creek to Joseph Creek)
  Scenic: 4.4 miles (Joseph Creek to mouth)

State Scenic River: the Grande Ronde River has been studied and recommended for designation as a state scenic river.
Special Values: The Grande Ronde River snakes through a canyon cut 2,000 feet into a plateau built up by flow after flow of basalt. It is the most outstanding example of an arid, rock-walled river canyon in Washington. A premier rafting and kayaking river, it is boatable from April through July. The Grande Ronde River hosts salmon and steelhead, with the rapid restoration of

Palouse River Canyon, Palouse Falls State Park

the steelhead runs providing a major sport fishery. The canyon provides important winter game habitat and has numerous Indian cultural sites as well as a long history of mining and ranching by the many immigrants who settled the area. The Oregon portion was designated Wild and Scenic in 1988.

■   **JOSEPH CREEK**
Tributary of: Grande Ronde River
Outstandingly Remarkable Values: Geology, history
Threats: Poor grazing practices
Segments & Classification
   Wild: 3.4 miles (Oregon border to Cottonwood Creek)
   Scenic: 4.5 miles (Cottonwood Creek to mouth)
Special Values: The creek has cut deeply into the volcanic rock; it is a superlative example of a rejuvenated stream erosion process and provides a classic example of "gooseneck" meanders. The creek valley is the ancestral home of Chief Joseph and the Nez Perce tribe.

■   **NORTH FORK WENAHA RIVER**
Tributary of: Wenaha River which flows into Grande Ronde River
Outstandingly Remarkable Values: Fish, wildlife, scenery
Threats: None
Segments & Classification
   Wild: 12 miles (source to confluence with Wenaha River)
Special Values: The main Wenaha River was designated as a wild river in the Oregon Omnibus Wild and Scenic Rivers Act of 1988. The whole river system provides outstanding habitat for trout, deer and elk, and other native Blue Mountain species in an undisturbed setting. The river valley has outstanding scenic views of the Blue Mountains.

■   **SNAKE RIVER**
Tributary of: Columbia River
Outstandingly Remarkable Values: Fish, wildlife, recreation,

scenery, history, culture
Threats: Unmanaged recreation, mining, grazing
Segments & Classification
   Scenic: 11 miles (from lower end of Wild and Scenic Snake River to mouth of Grande Ronde River)
   Recreation: 22 miles (from Grande Ronde to Asotin)
Special Values: This section includes the lower end of Hells Canyon, the deepest river canyon in the United States. It has important runs of salmon and steelhead, golden eagles, winter game range, mountain sheep, the termination of two of the most outstanding overnight wilderness whitewater rafting and kayaking trips in the United States, numerous Indian cultural sites, and many points of historical significance.

■   **TUCANNON RIVER**
Tributary of: Snake River
Outstandingly Remarkable Values: Fish, wildlife, scenery
Threats: Potential gold mining on national forest lands
Segments & Classification
   Wild: 7.8 miles (source to Sheep Creek)
   Scenic: 6.8 miles (Sheep Creek to Little Tucannon)
   Recreation: 9.5 miles (Little Tucannon to Cummings Creek)
Special Values: Important elk habitat, good runs of salmon and steelhead, valuable trout fishery, much use of the valley for hiking and hunting, spectacular views of the Blue Mountains.

■   **PALOUSE RIVER**
Tributary of: Snake River
Outstandingly Remarkable Values: Scenery, geology
Threats: Recent hydroelectric applications
Segments & Classification
   Scenic: 7 miles (Gildersleeve Falls to mouth)
Special Values: This section of the Palouse flows through a dramatic, vertical-walled canyon cut through Columbia basalt. Both the Little Palouse and Palouse falls (185-foot vertical drop) provide dramatic punctuation to this spectacular desert canyon.

■ **COLUMBIA RIVER (Hanford Reach)**
Tributary of: Pacific Ocean
Outstandingly Remarkable Values: Last free-flowing stretch of the Columbia left in the U.S., fish, wildlife, culture
Segments & Classification
   Recreation: 55 miles (from Priest Rapids Dam downstream to slack water at McNary Pool)

State Scenic River: The Hanford Reach has been studied and recommended for designation as a state scenic river.
Special Values: The Hanford Reach provides the most diverse fish and wildlife habitat on the mid-Columbia. The area is used by bald eagles, peregrine falcons, Canada geese, chinook and coho salmon, and steelhead, to mention just a few. The area is blessed with a large number of known archaeological sites.

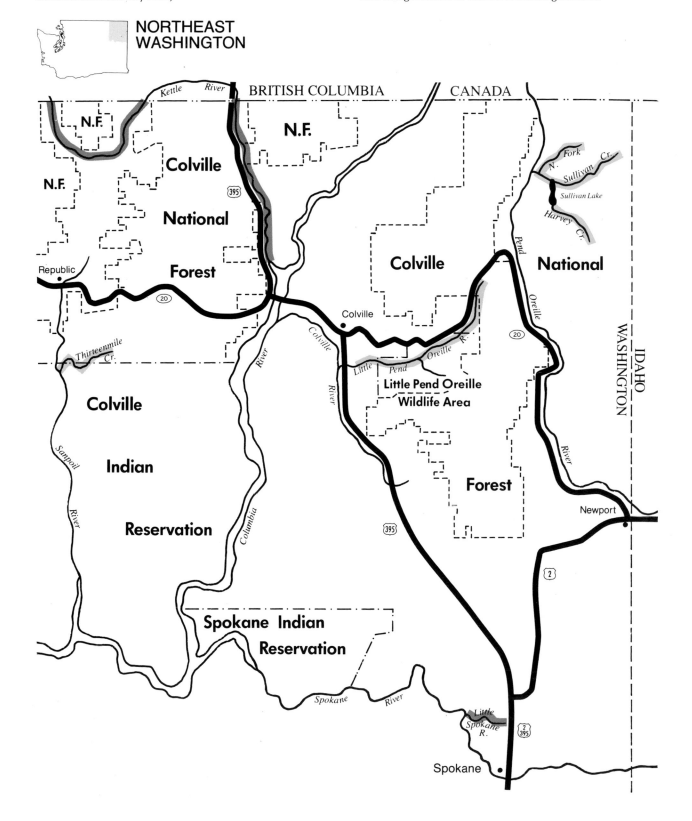

NORTHEAST WASHINGTON

■ KETTLE RIVER

Tributary of: Columbia River
Outstandingly Remarkable Values: Scenery, recreation, fish, history
Threats: Revived gold mining could harm water quality
Segments & Classification
   State Scenic River: The Kettle River has been studied and recommended for designation as a state scenic river.
Special Values: The Kettle River has a beautiful winding course through open fields and ponderosa pine covered hills. It offers many opportunities for both flat-water and whitewater boating and has a blue-ribbon trout fishery along with historic mining sites.

■ LITTLE PEND OREILLE RIVER

Tributary of: Colville River
Outstandingly Remarkable Values: Wildlife, recreation
Threats: No current threats
Segments & Classification
   Recreational: 8 miles (Coffin Lake to Prospect Creek)
   Scenic: 16 miles (Prospect Creek to Arden)
Special Values: The Little Pend Oreille offers wonderful canoeing and kayaking as well as important wildlife habitat; punctuated by scenic Crystal Falls.

■ SULLIVAN CREEK

Tributary of: Pend Oreille River
Outstandingly Remarkable Values: Fish, wildlife, recreation
Threats: No current threats
Segments & Classification
   Wild: 3.5 miles (source to Salmo Mountain Road)
   Wild: 8 miles (North Fork Sullivan Creek)
   Scenic: 15 miles (Salmo Mountain Road to outlet from Sullivan Lake)
Special Values: Sullivan Creek is a very important recreational area for northeast Washington, supporting important wildlife habitat areas and a native west slope cutthroat trout fishery.

■ HARVEY CREEK

Tributary of: Sullivan Lake
Outstandingly Remarkable Values: Fish, wildlife
Threats: No current threats
Segments & Classification
   Scenic: 8.5 miles (Bunchgrass Lake to Rocky Fork)
Special Values: Valuable fish and wildlife habitat.

■ THIRTEENMILE CREEK

Tributary of: Sanpoil River
Outstandingly Remarkable Values: Scenery, wildlife
Threats: Logging and road-building
Segments & Classification
   Wild: 8 miles (source to leaving Colville Reservation)
   Scenic: 3 miles (leaving Colville Reservation to mouth)
Special Values: Spectacular undisturbed pine forest and meadows, important wildlife habitat.

■ LITTLE SPOKANE RIVER

Tributary of: Spokane River
Outstandingly Remarkable Values: Wildlife, recreation
Threats: Encroaching housing development

Segments & Classification
   State Scenic River: 6 miles (from Waikiki Road to mouth of the Little Spokane has been studied and recommended for addition to the state scenic program.)
Special Values: The Little Spokane provides wonderful wildlife habitat just outside of Spokane. Blue herons, deer, and woodpeckers inhabit an old river channel area which makes for a fine canoe trip.

YAKIMA RIVER BASIN

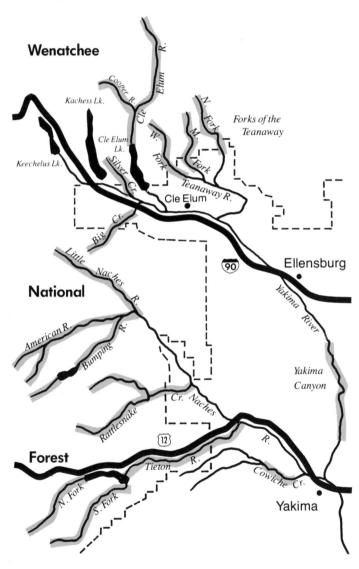

■ TIETON RIVER

Tributary of: Naches River
Outstandingly Remarkable Values: Recreation, geology, wildlife, scenery
Threats: Unmanaged recreational use
Segments & Classification
   Wild: 6 miles (source of South Fork to Long Creek)

Scenic: 11 miles (South Fork from Long Creek to Rimrock Lake)

Wild: 7 miles (source of North Fork to Scatter Creek)

Scenic: 5 miles (North Fork from Scatter Creek to Clear Lake)

Recreation: 21 miles (Rimrock Dam to mouth)

Special Values: The Tieton reveals the remnants of old volcanoes and volcanic intrusions amid pine-forest and desert-scrub scenery. It is one of the most heavily used whitewater rafting rivers in the state because it offers good whitewater in September when other rivers are nearly dried up. The rock-outcroppings punctuate beautiful "dry side" scenery. The North and South forks provide important wildlife habitat amid beautiful scenery, particularly the Conrad meadows, Minnie meadows, and Tieton meadow.

■ RATTLESNAKE CREEK

Tributary of: Naches River

Outstandingly Remarkable Values: Fish, wildlife, ecology

Threats: Proposed water supply dam

Segments & Classification

Wild: 16 miles (source to Little Rattlesnake Creek)

Special Values: Significant bull trout fishery amid a high variety of ecosystems up and down the drainage. The area supports Rocky Mountain elk, mule deer, and unusual habitats such as cliffs and rims along the river and deciduous woodlands in an otherwise arid environment.

■ BUMPING RIVER

Tributary of: American River

Outstandingly Remarkable Values: Fish, wildlife, ecology

Threats: Water-supply dam

Segments & Classification

Wild: 8 miles (source to Bumping Lake)

Scenic: 12 miles (Bumping Lake Dam to American River)

Special Values: The Bumping River has a good trout fishery; is inhabited by bull trout; and has good potential for restoration of Chinook salmon and steelhead. The mature, old growth and the riparian vegetation provide important wildlife habitat, particularly for Rocky Mountain elk, mule deer, bald eagles, and peregrine falcons. An unusually high water table creates an important ecological area in which western red cedar is the dominant tree.

■ AMERICAN RIVER

Tributary of: Naches River

Outstandingly Remarkable Values: Scenery, ecology

Threats: No current threats

Segments & Classification

Wild: 6 miles (American Lake to Rainier Fork)

Scenic: 26 miles (source of Rainier Fork to mouth)

Special Values: The American River flows through a wide variety of ecosystems in a spectacular valley ranging from alpine rock and meadows to deep old-growth forest. Steelhead and spring chinook salmon spawn in the same cold, clear water that provides a challenging run for expert kayakers. Bull trout and other resident fish inhabit the river, and bald eagles and peregrine falcons find habitat in the watershed.

■ LITTLE NACHES RIVER

Tributary of: Naches River

Outstandingly Remarkable Values: History, culture

Threats: Water-supply dam

Segments & Classification

Wild: 6 miles (source of North Fork to Blowout Creek)

Scenic: 5 miles (Blowout Creek to Pileup Creek)

Recreational: 6 miles (Pileup Creek to mouth)

Special Values: The route up the Little Naches and over Naches Pass was very heavily used both by the Indians and by early white settlers. It was the route taken by the Ezra Meeker party to Puget Sound, and it was also used by numerous cattle drives, military expeditions, and wagon trains.

■ COWICHE CREEK

Tributary of: Naches River

Outstandingly Remarkable Values: Recreation, wildlife, culture

Threats: Real estate development

Segments & Classification

Wild: 3 miles (Weikel to bridge in T 13 N, R 18 E, Section 18)

Special Values: Cowiche Canyon is an outstanding natural recreation area right on the outskirts of Yakima. An abandoned railroad right-of-way provides an excellent hiking trail through the canyon, which was used by Indians and now provides prime wildlife habitat.

■ YAKIMA RIVER

Tributary of: Columbia River

Outstandingly Remarkable Values: Recreation, geology, fish

Threats: Unmanaged recreational use, over-grazing

Segments & Classification

Recreation: 17 miles (from railroad bridge below Thrall to Selah Creek)

Special Values: The spectacular canyon of the Yakima River is geologically fascinating, displaying entrenched meanders cutting through layers of folded basalt. This section of the Yakima is one of the most heavily used rivers in the state for float trips. It also provides one of the state's most outstanding recreational trout fisheries.

■ FORKS OF THE TEANAWAY

Tributary of: Yakima River

Outstandingly Remarkable Values: Scenery, ecology, wildlife

Threats: Road building, logging on Middle and West forks

Segments & Classification

Wild: 8 miles (source of West Fork Teanaway River to Corral Creek)

Wild: 12 miles (source of Middle Fork Teanaway River to bridge in T 21 N, R 15 E, Section 21)

Wild: 2 miles (source of North Fork Teanaway River to end of North Fork road)

Scenic: 10 miles (North Fork Teanaway River, road end to Jungle Creek)

Special Values: The North Fork Teanaway River provides access to an incomparable recreational area, providing fishing, hiking, hunting, and camping in a beautiful mountain valley. It also has important ecological value because of the unusual plant communities associated with the serpentine rock outcroppings found there. The Middle and West forks provide outstanding undisturbed moderate-elevation wildlife habitat south of the Alpine Lakes Wilderness. Particularly important is the value of these river valleys as migration corridors for deer and elk.

■ **SILVER CREEK**
Tributary of: Yakima River
Outstandingly Remarkable Values: Scenery, geology
Threats: No current threats
Segments & Classification
   Wild: 6 miles (source to end of road in T 21 N, R 13 E, Section 35)
Special Values: Silver Creek cascades out of a hanging valley in a spectacular waterfall. The undisturbed upper valley has old-growth forest, fine wildlife habitat, and primitive recreational opportunities.

■ **CLE ELUM RIVER**
Tributary of: Yakima River
Outstandingly Remarkable Values: Scenery, recreation, history, culture
Threats: Placer mining
Segments & Classification
   Wild: 4 miles (source to Skeeter Creek)
   Wild: 3 miles (source of Cooper River to Wilderness boundary)
   Scenic: 20.5 miles (Skeeter Creek to Lake Cle Elum)
   Scenic: 9 miles (Cooper river from Wilderness boundary to mouth)
Special Values: This area has very high cultural significance for the Yakima Indians, providing salmon fishing and huckleberry gathering grounds as well as access over Deception Pass to the Skykomish country. It is a very scenic valley, with riffles, cascades, and deep pools framed by old-growth forest. A very heavily used recreational area, the river provides moderate whitewater for canoeists, rafters, and kayakers, and an expert kayak run above Salmon La Sac. There are numerous historical sites: mining claims, cabins, and the Salmon La Sac Guard Station, which is on the National Register of Historical Places. The Cooper River has substantial old growth, which provides important wildlife habitat and significant ecological diversity, as well as opportunities for kayaking.

■ **BIG CREEK**
Tributary of: Yakima River
Outstandingly Remarkable Values: Scenery, ecology
Threats: Logging
Segments & Classification
   Scenic: 4 miles (source to confluence with Greek Creek)
   Wild: 5 miles (Greek Creek to powerline in T 20 N, R 14 E, Section 29)
Special Values: Big Creek flows through a deep gorge lined with beautiful arid-transition zone forest. The virgin forest provides important ecological diversity and wildlife habitat in an area that has been traversed by roads and heavily logged.

WENATCHEE & ENTIAT BASINS

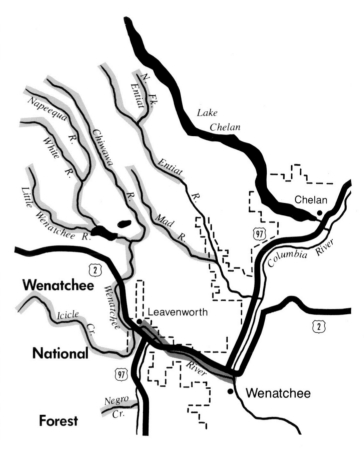

■ **ICICLE CREEK**
Tributary of: Wenatchee River
Outstandingly Remarkable Values: Scenery, recreation
Threats: No current threats
Segments & Classification
   Wild: 12 miles (source to Grindstone Creek)
   Scenic: 15 miles (Grindstone Creek to Snow Creek)
Special Values: Icicle Creek flows through a dramatic, granite mountain valley that is heavily used for camping, hiking, and mountain climbing. The creek rushes down steep cascades, around boulders, and through dense forest.

■ **NEGRO CREEK**
Tributary of: Peshastin Creek
Outstandingly Remarkable Values: History, ecology
Threats: Off-road-vehicle use could harm rare plants
Segments & Classification
   Scenic: 8 miles (source to mouth)
Special Values: The upper end has big meadows and mountain views while the middle portion is in a deep gorge. A very rare plant, *Silene seelyi* (a relative of the carnation), is found along the banks. There are old mine sites and an abandoned mine road visible in places.

■ **WENATCHEE RIVER**

Tributary of: Columbia River
Outstandingly Remarkable Values: Scenery, recreation, fish, history, culture, ecology
Threats: Shoreline development
Segments & Classification

Recreation: 25 miles (Lake Wenatchee to national forest boundary)
State Scenic River: The Wenatchee has been studied and recommended for designation as a state scenic river.

Special Values: Forming part of this river section, spectacular Tumwater Canyon is heavily used for picnicking, camping, and photography. This section of river provides an important passageway for anadromous fish to the Little Wenatchee, White, and Chiwawa rivers. The river was also an important travel corridor for the Wenatchee Indians and contains numerous archaeological sites and the only known petroglyph site in the Wenatchee National Forest. Historically, the river is a site of early placer mining, railroad construction and hydroelectric generation. Within the river corridor is the Tumwater Botanical Area, which protects plants unique to this area.

■ **LITTLE WENATCHEE RIVER**

Tributary of: Wenatchee River
Outstandingly Remarkable Values: Fish, scenery
Threats: Logging
Segments & Classification

Wild: 6 miles (source to Wilderness boundary)
Scenic: 21.5 miles (Wilderness boundary to mouth)
Wild: 3 miles (source of Lake Creek to road end)
Scenic: 3 miles (Lake Creek from road end to Little Wenatchee)

Special Values: The Little Wenatchee River is home to five runs of anadromous fish: steelhead, sockeye salmon, silver salmon, and spring and fall chinook salmon. It is one of only four rivers in Eastern Washington with a sockeye salmon run. Lake Creek has a large volume of water rushing over cascades and waterfalls. Its valley is of high value for dispersed, primitive recreation.

■ **WHITE RIVER**

Tributary of: Wenatchee River
Outstandingly Remarkable Values: Scenery, fish
Threats: Shoreline development
Segments & Classification

Wild: 15 miles (source to Wilderness boundary)
Scenic: 19 miles (Wilderness boundary to mouth)

Special Values: The river corridor includes glaciers, snowfields, rocky steep slopes, cascading water, riffles, rapids, and some significant falls. Along the bank are a considerable number of old growth trees of species more typical of Western than Eastern Washington. There is much recreational use of the area, part of which is associated with the fishing. Five runs of anadromous fish spawn in the river, which is one of only four in Eastern Washington with a sockeye-salmon run.

■ **NAPEEQUA RIVER**

Tributary of: White River
Outstandingly Remarkable Values: Scenery, geology
Threats: No current threats
Segments & Classification

Wild: 15 miles (source to Wilderness boundary)

Scenic: 1 mile (Wilderness boundary to mouth)
Special Values: The drainage is characterized by peaks, snowfields, glaciers, and glaciated valleys with waterfalls, cascades, and meandering water. It also has meadows, scattered old growth trees, and mixed forest with hardwoods.

■ **CHIWAWA RIVER**

Tributary of: Wenatchee River
Outstandingly Remarkable Values: Scenery, recreation, fish
Threats: Combined hydroelectric and water-supply dam
Segments & Classification

Wild: 5 miles (source to Wilderness boundary)
Scenic: 26.5 miles (Wilderness boundary to south end of T 27 N, R 18 E, Section 30)
Recreational: 2.5 miles (south end of T 27 N, R 18 E, Section 30 to mouth)
Wild: 7 miles (source of Raging Creek to Chiwawa River)
Scenic: 3 miles (source of Chikamin Creek to south end of T 29 N, R 17 E, Section 27)
Wild: 4 miles (Chikamin Creek from south end of T 29 N, R 17 E, Section 29 to Marble Creek)
Scenic: 1 mile (Chikamin Creek from Marble Creek to mouth)

Special Values: The Chiwawa is a prime recreational river. It has fine family camping areas, slow water for canoeing above Chickamin Creek, and whitewater for rafting and kayaking below Chickamin. The Chiwawa has old-growth forest all along its west bank above Chickamin Creek, and beautiful peaks, glaciers, and snowfields in its upper valley. The river also supports four runs of anadromous fish and excellent fishing for trout. Raging Creek and Chikamin Creek have fine trout in undisturbed and little-disturbed side valleys.

■ **MAD RIVER**

Tributary of: Entiat River
Outstandingly Remarkable Values: Recreation, fish, ecology
Threats: Logging, off-road-vehicle damage to ecological values
Segments & Classification

Wild: 21 miles (source—Mad Lake—to Pine Flat Campground)
Scenic: 2 miles (Pine Flat Campground to Tillicum Creek)
Wild: 5 miles (source of Hornet Creek to Mad River)

Special Values: Trail #1409, which follows the Mad River, is the longest low-elevation trail in the forest, extensively used by hikers, hunters, anglers, and campers. The Mad supports anadromous fish as well as bull trout, a rare species. There is a wide variety of ecosystems along the river and at least one rare plant species is found here. Hornet Creek flows through an undisturbed area, which has been proposed as a Research Natural Area.

■ **ENTIAT AND NORTH FORK ENTIAT**

Tributary of: Columbia River
Outstandingly Remarkable Values: Scenery, ecology, geology
Threats: Logging, road building
Segments & Classification

Wild: 16.5 miles (source of main river to Cottonwood)
Scenic: 15 miles (Cottonwood to Burns Creek)
Wild: 8 miles (source of North Fork Entiat River to bridge above mouth)

Special Values: The drainage contains spectacular views of mountain peaks, glacially sculpted valleys, and beautiful meadows. The North Fork flows through a narrow canyon in its lower reaches and the main Entiat River flows through a classic box canyon in the lower portion of the scenic segment. As the river descends from over 7,000 feet in elevation to under 2,000 feet, it passes through a wide variety of ecosystems.

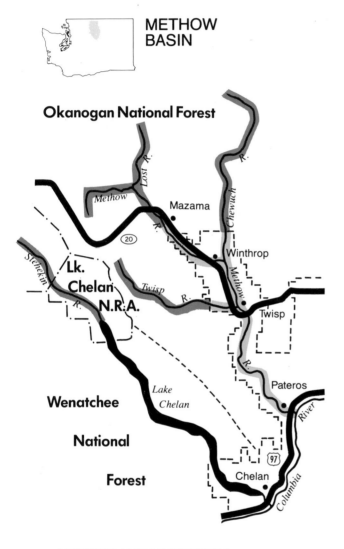

METHOW BASIN

Okanogan National Forest

Lost R.

Methow

Mazama

20

Chewuch R.

Winthrop

Stehekin R.

Lk. Chelan N.R.A.

Twisp R.

Methow R.

Twisp

Wenatchee

Lake Chelan

National

Pateros

Columbia River

97

Forest

Chelan

■   **METHOW AND LOST RIVERS**
Tributary of: Columbia River
Outstandingly Remarkable Values: Scenery, wildlife, fish, geology, history
Threats: Shoreline development, logging
Segments & Classification
   Wild: 17 miles (source of Methow River to Rattlesnake Creek)
   Scenic: 12 miles (Rattlesnake Creek to Goat Creek)
   Wild: 20 miles (source of Lost River to bridge on Forest Road 5400)
   Scenic: 0.5 mile (bridge on Forest Road 5400 to mouth)
   State Scenic River: The Methow has been studied and recommended for designation as a state scenic river.
Special Values: Both the main Methow and the Lost rivers have spectacular valleys. The Methow exhibits a classic U-shaped valley, the north wall of which is known as the "Goat Wall" for

the frequent sighting of mountain goats there. The valley is still largely undisturbed above Early Winters. The Lost River has carved a dazzling gorge through pink granite as it cuts its way out of the Pasayten Wilderness to join the Methow. Salmon and steelhead run all the way up the Methow to Rattlesnake Creek, and up the Lost into the Lost River Gorge. These valleys are home to the largest mule deer herd in the state and contain numerous old mines and early settler's cabins of historical value.

■   **TWISP RIVER**
Tributary of: Methow River
Outstandingly Remarkable Values: Scenery, wildlife, recreation
Threats: Logging, mining
Segments & Classification
   Wild: 4 miles (source of North Fork Twisp to end of road)
   Scenic: 20 miles (end of road to Poorman Creek)
   State Scenic River: The Twisp was studied and recommended along with the Methow for designation as a state scenic river.
Special Values: The Twisp provides important habitat for deer and mountain goats as well as being heavily used for camping, picnicking, hiking, and fishing. The upper part of the valley offers dramatic views of the mountains in the Chelan-Sawtooth Wilderness.

■   **CHEWUCH RIVER**
Tributary of: Methow River
Outstandingly Remarkable Values: Recreation, fish, wildlife
Threats: Logging, road building
Segments & Classification
   Wild: 12 miles (source to Wilderness boundary)
   Scenic: 25 miles (Wilderness boundary to Boulder Creek)
   State Scenic River: The Chewuch, along with the Methow and Twisp rivers, has been studied and recommended for designation as a state scenic river.
Special Values: The Chewuch is a fine recreational river with numerous camps for families, whitewater rapids for rafters and kayakers, and good fishing holes for fishermen. Salmon and steelhead return to the upper Chewuch to spawn, and many species of wildlife inhabit the valley.

■   **STEHEKIN RIVER**
Tributary of: Lake Chelan
Outstandingly Remarkable Values: Recreation, scenery, history, culture
Threats: Riprapping, sand and gravel mining
Segments & Classification
   Wild: 3 miles (source to Cottonwood)
   Scenic: 19 miles (Cottonwood to mouth)
Special Values: The Stehekin is the most undisturbed major river valley on the east side of the Cascades. The Indians long used the valley as a trading route, and miners came to the valley in the late nineteenth century. The Stehekin offers outstanding scenic views of the surrounding mountains and has unparalleled primitive recreational opportunities such as hiking, camping, kayaking, rafting, and fishing.

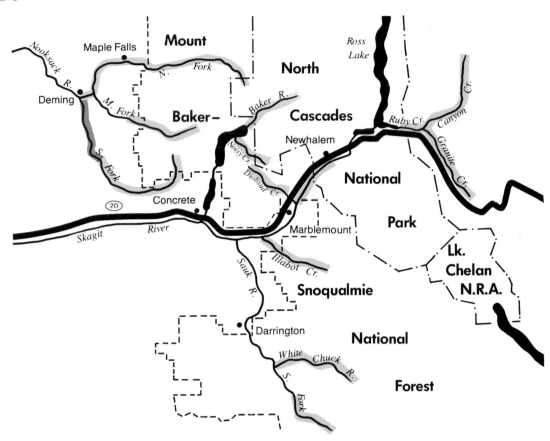

■ NORTH FORK NOOKSACK RIVER

Tributary of: Nooksack River
Outstandingly Remarkable Values: Recreation, geology, fish, wildlife
Threats: Hydroelectric development, logging
Segments & Classification
  Wild: 6 miles (source to White Salmon Creek)
  Scenic: 37 miles (White Salmon Creek to South Fork Nooksack River)
  Wild: 4 miles (Wells Creek Source to Forest Road 33 bridge)
  Scenic: 4 miles (Wells Creek from bridge on Forest Road 33 to mouth)
  State Scenic River: The North Fork Nooksack River has been studied and recommended for designation as a state scenic river.
Special Values: The North Fork has deep gorges, spectacular Nooksack Falls, and headwaters in the stunning Nooksack Cirque. It is home to all species of salmon and steelhead and provides habitat for bald eagles. It also supports a good Dolly Varden fishery. Wells Creek is an important part of the North Fork ecosystem, providing nutrients for fish and important wildlife habitat. The North Fork Nooksack provides fine boating, kayaking above Douglas Fir Camp, whitewater rafting from the Camp to Maple Falls, and flat-water floating below Maple Falls. It, the Suiattle, and the Skagit rivers are the only ones in Washington to provide whitewater boating in August.

■ MIDDLE FORK NOOKSACK

Tributary of: North Fork Nooksack River
Outstandingly Remarkable Values: Fish, wildlife
Threats: Logging, mining
Segments & Classification
  Wild: 3 miles (source to Wilderness boundary)
  Scenic: 9 miles (Wilderness to diversion dam below Falls Creek)
  Recreation: 2 miles (diversion dam to Heisler's Creek)
Special Values: The Middle Fork Nooksack River provides spawning and rearing habitat for chinook, coho, chum, and pink salmon. It also provides habitat for numerous wildlife species, including bald eagles.

■ SOUTH FORK NOOKSACK

Tributary of: Nooksack River
Outstandingly Remarkable Values: Fish, wildlife
Threats: Logging, road building
Segments & Classification
  Scenic: 23 miles (source to Cavanaugh Creek)
  State Scenic River: The South Fork has been studied and recommended for designation as a state scenic river.
Special Values: The South Fork Nooksack River provides spawning and rearing habitat for chinook, coho, pink and some chum salmon; it is the main spawning grounds for spring chinook in the Nooksack drainage. It also provides important wildlife habi-

tat, a flora unique to outcroppings of serpentine rock, and a moderately difficult wilderness whitewater trip from near Lyman Pass to Saxon bridge.

■   **BAKER RIVER**
Tributary of: Skagit River
Outstandingly Remarkable Values: Scenery, fish, wildlife
Threats: No current threats
Segments & Classification
   Wild: 13 miles (source to Blum Creek)
   Scenic: 2 miles (Blum Creek to Baker Lake)
Special Values: Very rare undisturbed, low elevation Cascade river valley. Chinook, coho, and sockeye salmon spawn in the Baker River, and there is a fine Dolly Varden fishery. Spotted owls, deer, bear, and beaver find habitat in the Baker River valley.

■   **NOISY CREEK**
Tributary of: Baker River (Baker Lake)
Outstandingly Remarkable Values: Wildlife, ecology
Threats: Proposed hydro project and power line corridor
Segments & Classification
   Wild: 6 miles (source to mouth)
Special Values: Outstanding low elevation old-growth forest provides important wildlife habitat and protection of rare ecological values. Known spotted owl nesting and forage site and native trout fishery.

■   **DIOBSUD CREEK**
Tributary of: Skagit River
Outstandingly Remarkable Values: Recreation, wildlife
Threats: Proposed hydroelectric project
Segments & Classification
   Wild: 9 miles (source to east end of Section 25, T 36 N, R 10 E)
   Scenic: 1.8 miles (from Section 25 to mouth)
Special Values: Beautiful hiking trail through old-growth forest and then through steep-walled canyon. Snags and other habitat features of undisturbed forest; lowest elevation stream eligible for Wild River designation in the Cascade Range.

■   **RUBY CREEK**
Tributary of: Skagit River (Ross Lake)
Outstandingly Remarkable Values: Recreation, scenery, wildlife
Threats: Hydroelectric development, mining
Segments & Classification
   Wild: 17 miles (source of Canyon Creek to mouth)
   Scenic: 23 miles (source of Granite Creek to Ruby Creek)
   Recreational: 5 miles (source of Ruby Creek to mouth)
Special Values: Ruby and Granite creeks offer outstanding views of the rugged North Cascades. Both Ruby and Granite also provide excellent kayak runs on pristine waters. Canyon Creek offers outstanding scenery from the trail which parallels it nearly to its headwaters. It provides important undisturbed habitat adjacent to the higher Pasayten Wilderness.

■   **SKAGIT RIVER**
Tributary of: Puget Sound
Outstandingly Remarkable Values: Fish, wildlife, recreation
Threats: Copper Creek Dam
Segments & Classification
   Scenic: 11 miles (Newhalem Creek to Bacon Creek)

Special Values: The section of the Skagit above Bacon Creek enjoys no Wild and Scenic protection. Rather, as part of the Ross Lake National Recreation Area adjacent to North Cascades National Park, it would be inundated were Seattle City Light ever to proceed with the construction of the proposed Copper Creek Dam. Yet this section of the river has outstanding rafting and kayaking, runs of salmon, and beautiful scenery.

■   **ILLABOT CREEK**
Tributary of: Skagit River
Outstandingly Remarkable Values: Fish, wildlife
Threats: Logging
Segments & Classification
   Wild: 4 miles (source to Wilderness boundary)
   Scenic: 11 miles (Wilderness boundary to mouth)
Special Values: Illabot Creek has fine runs of chinook, coho, chum, and pink salmon and provides very important bald eagle habitat, with several known nesting and roosting sites.

■   **WHITE CHUCK RIVER**
Tributary of: Sauk River
Outstandingly Remarkable Values: Scenery, recreation, fish, wildlife
Threats: Hydroelectric development
Segments & Classification
   Wild: 10 miles (source to Wilderness boundary)
   Scenic: 12 miles (Wilderness boundary to mouth)
Special Values: Provides spawning areas for spring chinook and coho. Stunning mountain views, extensive use for dispersed, primitive recreation. Kayak run on lower six miles. Important old-growth forest and undisturbed wildlife habitat.

■   **SOUTH FORK SAUK RIVER EXTENSION**
Tributary of: Skagit River
Outstandingly Remarkable Values: Scenery, fish, history, wildlife
Threats: Gold mining
Segments & Classification
   Wild: 2.5 miles (source to Glacier Creek)
   Scenic: 8.5 miles (Glacier Creek to Elliott Creek)
Special Values: The river below Elliott Creek is already designated as Wild and Scenic. The Upper South Fork Sauk provides spawning areas for spring chinook, coho, and pink salmon. There are also fine Dolly Varden in the pools in the headwaters. The ghost town of Monte Cristo and nearby remains of old mines are of significant historical interest. There is fine wildlife habitat, and there have been some sightings of spotted owls. The river corridor lies along the Mountain Loop Highway and offers dramatic views of the North Cascades.

STILLAGUAMISH, SNOHOMISH, & DUWAMISH BASINS

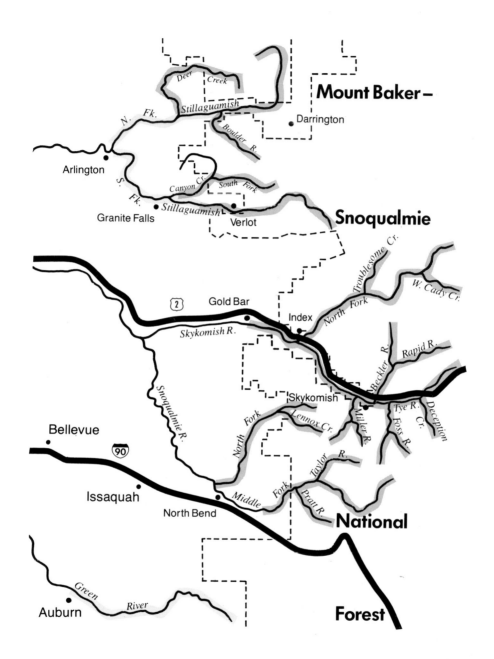

■ NORTH FORK STILLAGUAMISH

Tributary of: Stillaguamish River

Outstandingly Remarkable Values: Fish, wildlife

Threats: Logging

Segments & Classification

> *Scenic:* 28.5 miles (source of North Branch Stillaguamish River to Boulder River)
>
> *Wild:* 7 miles (source of Bolder River to Boulder Falls)
>
> *Scenic:* 4 miles (Boulder River from Boulder Falls to mouth)
>
> *State Scenic River:* The North Fork Stillaguamish River has

been studied and recommended for designation as a state scenic river.

Special Values: Large numbers of chinook, pink, and chum salmon spawn in the main stem of the river, while coho use the accessible tributaries, such as Squire Creek. The North Fork is a major steelhead river, with extensive recreational use downstream. The mixed hardwood and coniferous forest along the river provides important wildlife habitat for this area northwest of Darrington. From South Branch of the North Fork down is a kayak run.

■ **DEER CREEK**
Tributary of: North Fork Stillaguamish River
Outstandingly Remarkable Values: Fish, wildlife
Threats: Logging
Segments & Classification
   Scenic: 22 miles (source to tributary creek at about mile 2)
Special Values: Deer Creek provides spawning and rearing habitat for fall chinook, spring chinook, and coho salmon and is accessible to anadromous fish nearly to its headwaters. The creek is also home of the legendary run of summer steelhead written about by Zane Gray. Since Gray's time, the steelhead have greatly diminished in numbers due to extensive logging in the drainage, but they may be able to rebound if the drainage is protected. The upper part of the watershed contains three spotted owl habitat areas, and the lower 11 miles provide a kayak run.

■ **SOUTH FORK STILLAGUAMISH**
Tributary of: Stillaguamish River
Outstandingly Remarkable Values: Scenery, recreation, fish, wildlife, history, ecology
Threats: Shoreline development, gold mining
Segments & Classification
   Scenic: 36 miles (source to Granite Falls—river feature, not town)
   State Scenic River: The South Fork Stillaguamish River has been studied and recommended for designation as a state scenic river.
Special Values: The South Fork Stillaguamish valley has dramatic views of the surrounding mountains and offers an interesting river channel studded with boulders. There is easy whitewater paddling above Boardman Creek, and moderately difficult whitewater from Boardman Creek downstream to Verlot. There are several spotted owl habitat areas in the upper watershed, and the river has important runs of chinook, coho, chum, and pink salmon. The old mining towns and abandoned mining railroad to Monte Cristo offer historical interest.

■ **CANYON CREEK & SOUTH FORK CANYON CREEK**
Tributary of: South Fork Stillaguamish River
Outstandingly Remarkable Values: Fish, wildlife
Threats: Logging
Segments & Classification
   Wild: 2.5 miles (source of South Fork Canyon Creek to Wilderness boundary)
   Scenic: 12 miles (Wilderness boundary to creek just above river mile 6)
Special Values: Chinook and coho make some use of lower 13 miles of river. Spotted owl habitat exists near confluence with North Fork and in upper reaches of South Fork. The section of river proposed for Wild and Scenic designation hosts a kayak run in its lower few miles.

■ **NORTH FORK SKYKOMISH**
Tributary of: Skykomish River
Outstandingly Remarkable Values: Scenery, recreation, fish, wildlife
Threats: Hydroelectric projects, shoreline development
Segments & Classification
   Wild: 8 miles (source to Quartz Creek)
   Scenic: 8 miles (Quartz Creek to Troublesome Creek)
   Recreation: 12 miles (Troublesome Creek to mouth)
   Wild: 4 miles (West Cady Creek, from source to bridge over creek on Forest Road 6580)
   Scenic: 3 miles (West Cady Creek, from bridge on Forest Road 6580 to mouth)
   Wild: 4.5 miles (Troublesome Creek, from Lake Blanca to Forest Road 63)
Special Values: Already a state scenic river below Bear Creek Falls at river mile 13, the North Fork Skykomish River provides spawning habitat for large numbers of chinook and coho salmon, and steelhead. The fish not only spawn in the main river but migrate up into the lower ends of Troublesome Creek and West Cady Creek. From Bear Creek Falls down, the North Fork supports very popular kayaking and rafting runs. A great diversity of wildlife, including bald eagles, spotted owls, and mountain goats, make use of the North Fork, Troublesome Creek, and West Cady Creek drainages. The North Fork has a very scenic valley with spectacular views of Mount Index, Mount Persis, and Gunn Peak.

■ **SKYKOMISH RIVER & SOUTH FORK SKYKOMISH**
Tributary of: Snohomish River
Outstandingly Remarkable Values: Scenery, recreation, fish, wildlife, history
Threats: Hydroelectric projects, shoreline development
Segments & Classification
   Recreation: 41 miles (all of Tye River, South Fork Skykomish River, and main Skykomish River downstream to Duffey Creek at about river mile 42)
   Wild: 5 miles (source of Rapid River to Wilderness boundary)
   Scenic: 7 miles (Rapid River from Wilderness boundary to Beckler River)
   Recreation: 13 miles (Beckler River)
   Wild: 9 miles (Deception Creek from source to U.S. 2)
   Wild: 7 miles (source of East Fork Foss River to Wilderness boundary)
   Wild: 3.5 miles (West Fork Foss River from Delta Lake to Wilderness boundary)
   Scenic: 6 miles (Wilderness boundary on East and West Fork Foss rivers to main Foss River, and along main Foss River to mouth)
   Wild: 1.5 miles (East Fork Miller River from Lake Dorothy to Wilderness boundary)
   Wild: 2 miles (West Fork Miller from source to Wilderness boundary)
   Scenic: 12.5 miles (East Fork and West Fork Miller rivers from Wilderness boundary to main Miller River, and along main Miller River to mouth)
Special Values: The upper main Skykomish, the South Fork, and all of its tributaries form one large ecosystem with chinook and coho salmon migrating upstream into tributaries to spawn and wildlife migrating up and down the river corridors. Recreational boating runs begin on the Beckler, Tye, Foss, and Miller rivers and end on the South Fork. The main Skykomish, South Fork, Tye, and Beckler rivers are in the Washington State Scenic Rivers Program. There are spectacular mountain views from throughout the drainage. The South Fork and upper main Skykomish rivers provide the most difficult regularly run commercial rafting trip in the state. There are remnants of old towns and early railroads in the Tye drainage.

■ **NORTH FORK SNOQUALMIE RIVER**
Tributary of: Middle Fork Snoqualmie River
Outstandingly Remarkable Values: Fish, wildlife, recreation
Threats: Hydroelectric and water-supply dams
Segments & Classification
   Wild: 0.7 mile (source to Wilderness boundary)
   Scenic: 5 miles (Wilderness boundary to Lennox Creek)
   Recreation: 9.3 miles (Lennox Creek to Wagnor Bridge)
   Scenic: 11 miles (Wagnor Bridge to mouth)
Special Values: The North Fork Snoqualmie River has outstanding whitewater rafting and kayaking of a moderately difficult level. It is one of the Department of Wildlife's special high-quality trout-fishing rivers and provides critical winter range for deer.

■ **MIDDLE FORK SNOQUALMIE RIVER**
Tributary of: Snoqualmie River
Outstandingly Remarkable Values: Recreation, geology, fish, wildlife, ecology
Threats: Hydroelectric projects, shoreline development
Segments & Classification
   Wild: 5 miles (source to Wilderness boundary)
   Scenic: 29 miles (Wilderness boundary to Tanner)
   Wild: 8.9 miles (Taylor River from Snoqualmie Lake to Quartz Creek)
   Scenic: 1.1 miles (Taylor from Quartz Creek to mouth)
   Wild: 9 miles (Pratt River from source to mouth)
Special Values: The Middle Fork Snoqualmie River and its tributaries are a major recreational resource close to the Seattle metropolitan area. There are easy, moderately difficult, and difficult whitewater rafting and kayaking runs; high quality trout fishing; numerous areas for dispersed, primitive recreation; and many opportunities for camping and picnicking. The undisturbed forests in the upper Middle Fork, Pratt, and Taylor rivers provide critical winter wildlife habitat and spotted owl habitat, as well as scenic grandeur. A site on the lower Pratt River has the geologic curiosity known as "clay babies," natural clay formations in the shape of a baby doll.

■ **GREEN RIVER**
Tributary of: Duwamish River
Outstandingly Remarkable Values: Scenery, recreation, fish, history
Threats: Shoreline development, water diversion
Segments & Classification
   State Scenic River: The Green River from the Tacoma Water Headworks to Highway 18 (a distance of 29 miles) has been studied and recommended for designation as a state scenic river.
Special Values: The Green River flows through a spectacular gorge near Black Diamond and is one of the most highly valued recreational rivers in the state. It offers difficult and moderate whitewater runs for rafters and kayakers as well as easy floats for family canoeists. It also offers one of the best steelhead rivers on Puget Sound. Old abandoned mines and mining communities, such as the town of Franklin, add historical interest.

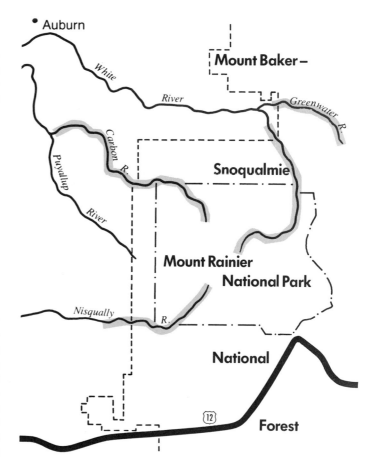

PUYALLUP & NISQUALLY BASINS

• Auburn

Mount Baker –

Snoqualmie

Mount Rainier National Park

National Forest

White River

Carbon R.

Puyallup River

Nisqually R.

Greenwater R.

■ **GREENWATER RIVER**
Tributary of: White River
Outstandingly Remarkable Values: Fish, wildlife, history
Threats: Road building
Segments & Classification
   Wild: 9.4 miles (source to Wilderness boundary)
   Recreation: 8 miles (from Wilderness boundary to creek below mile 4)
Special Values: The Greenwater River is one of the principal spawning areas for spring chinook in the Puyallup basin and serves moderate numbers of other chinook and coho. There is also good fishing for steelhead and both cutthroat and rainbow trout. Deer, elk, bald eagles, golden eagles, great egrets, and waterfowl make use of the Greenwater valley. The Ezra Meeker party, one of the first pioneer parties to settle on central Puget Sound, traveled down the Greenwater valley in the 1850s.

■ **WHITE RIVER**
Tributary of: Puyallup River
Outstandingly Remarkable Values: Recreation, fish, wildlife
Threats: Logging

Segments & Classification

Scenic: 25 miles (source to bridge at river mile 48, below West Fork)

Special Values: The White River provides habitat for spring chinook and coho salmon. It also has old-growth forest and provides important winter habitat for the wildlife of Mount Rainier National Park. The river below the West Fork is used extensively for whitewater rafting, and there is kayaking below Huckleberry Creek.

■ **CARBON RIVER**

Tributary of: Puyallup River
Outstandingly Remarkable Values: Scenery, fish
Threats: Hydroelectric project
Segments & Classification

Wild: 3.5 miles (Carbon Glacier to Ipsut Creek)
Scenic: 22.5 miles (Ipsut Creek to South Prairie Creek)
State Scenic River: The Carbon has been studied and

recommended for designation as a state scenic river.
Special Values: The Carbon River flows through one of the most spectacular gorges in the state near the small community of Fairfax. From the Fairfax bridge, you look down 200 feet to see the river foaming through a solid rock cleft. The rapids can be negotiated by fish, however, and chinook and coho salmon migrate up the gorge into Mount Rainier National Park.

■ **NISQUALLY RIVER**

Tributary of: Puget Sound
Outstandingly Remarkable Values: Geology, wildlife
Threats: Shoreline development
Segments & Classification

Scenic: 18 miles (Nisqually Glacier to Big Creek)
Special Values: The Nisqually River is a classic example of an Alaska-type glacier-fed stream. Its valley also provides essential low-elevation winter habitat for the wildlife of Mount Rainier National Park.

COWLITZ & LEWIS BASINS

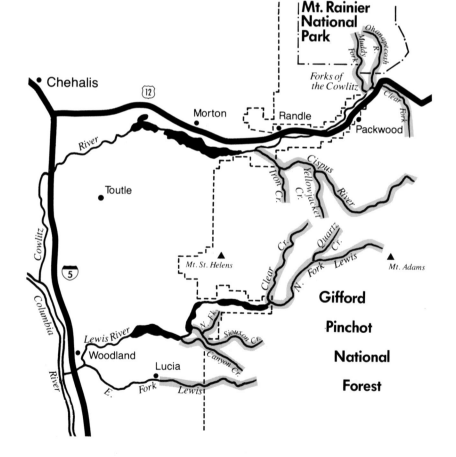

■ **FORKS OF THE COWLITZ**

Tributary of: Cowlitz River
Outstandingly Remarkable Values: Scenery, geology, culture
Threats: No current threats
Segments & Classification

Wild: 3 miles (source of Muddy Fork to Stevens Creek Road)
Scenic: 0.5 mile (Stevens Creek Road to Nickel Creek)

Wild: 8.5 miles (Nickel Creek to confluence with Clear Fork)
Wild: 6 miles (source of Ohanapecosh River to Chinook Creek)
Scenic: 11 miles (Ohanapecosh River from Chinook Creek to mouth)
Wild: 6 miles (source of Clear Fork Cowlitz River to Wilderness boundary)

Scenic: 9 miles (Wilderness boundary to confluence with Muddy Fork Cowlitz River)

Special Values: The Forks of the Cowlitz River offer an outstanding variety of scenery and interesting geological formations: a massive palisade of columnar basalt in the Ayance Canyon of the Clear Fork, an unusual boxlike gorge with a double 90-degree bend in the channel on the Muddy Fork, and a lush, rock-girt gorge on the Ohanapecosh. The area was of great cultural significance to the Indians, particularly the "Blue Hole" site at the confluence of the Clear Fork and the Ohanapecosh.

■ CISPUS RIVER

Tributary of: Cowlitz River
Outstandingly Remarkable Values: Scenery, fish, recreation, culture
Threats: Proposed hydroelectric projects on lower river
Segments & Classification
  Wild: 7 miles (source to Wilderness boundary)
  Scenic: 45 miles (Wilderness boundary to mouth)
  Scenic: 14 miles (source of Yellowjacket Creek to mouth)
  Scenic: 9 miles (source of Iron Creek to mouth)
  State Scenic River: The Cispus has been studied and recommended for designation as a state scenic river.

Special Values: The Cispus River has beautiful scenery, ranging from alpine meadows near the headwaters, through dramatic gorges in the mid-section of the river, to spectacular views of Tower Rock in the lower section. It also has some of the finest whitewater rafting and kayaking in the state along its lower 30 miles. There are also numerous Indian cultural sites. Iron Creek has an exciting kayak run through old-growth forest in its lower 2 to 3 miles. Yellowjacket Creek has some of the finest trout fishing in Southwest Washington.

Running the Drop at Smoothrock Falls, Cispus River, Gifford Pinchot National Forest

■ NORTH FORK LEWIS RIVER

Tributary of: Lewis River
Outstandingly Remarkable Values: Scenic, recreation, ecology, fish
Threats: Eagle Cliff Dam, logging, road building
Segments & Classification
  Wild: 4 miles (source to Wilderness boundary)
  Scenic: 31.5 miles (Wilderness boundary to Swift Reservoir)

  Wild: 8 miles (source of Quartz Creek to Straight Creek)
  Scenic: 2 miles (Quartz Creek from Straight Creek to mouth)
  Scenic: 5 miles (source of Clear Creek to Elk Creek)
  Wild: 7 miles (Clear Creek from Elk Creek to end of Forest Road 9303)
  Scenic: 4 miles (Clear Creek from end Forest Road 9303 to mouth)
  State Scenic River: The North Fork Lewis has been studied and recommended for designation as a state scenic river.

Special Values: Five falls on the main North Fork Lewis River, and numerous falls on the tributary creeks, make for spectacular scenery. The Washington Department of Wildlife manages this part of the Lewis as a quality recreational fishery. Quartz Creek has a genetically unique trout population—isolated above the Lewis River Falls for centuries. The North Fork, Clear Creek, and Quartz Creek are also bordered by some of the finest remaining old growth in the Gifford Pinchot National Forest. The North Fork has outstanding rafting and kayaking on its lower 13 miles and one of the finest riverside trails in the state. Spectacular scenery is found at the confluence of Clear Creek with Elk Creek—a deep pool in a grotto surrounded by old-growth forest.

■ SIOUXON CREEK

Tributary of: Yale Lake
Outstandingly Remarkable Values: Scenic, recreation, ecology
Threats: Logging, road building
Segments & Classification
  Wild: 15 miles (source to confluence with North Fork Siouxon Creek)
  Scenic: 2 miles (North Fork Siouxon Creek to Yale Lake)
  Wild: 7 miles (source of North Fork Siouxon to mouth)

Special Values: Outstanding natural second-growth forest (burned in the 1902 Yacolt fire) bordering pristine stream and followed by Siouxon trail for 10 miles. Excellent backcountry trout fishing.

■ CANYON CREEK

Tributary of: Merwin Lake
Outstandingly Remarkable Values: Scenery, recreation
Threats: Proposed hydroelectric project, logging
Segments & Classification
  Scenic: 19 miles (source—Zigzag Lake—to mouth)

Special Values: Canyon Creek flows through a spectacular gorge, lined by old-growth and mature forest within the national forest boundaries. Downstream from the forest boundary, the stream descends through a deep canyon, punctuated by a series of waterfalls, into Lake Merwin. Canyon Creek offers several challenging class 4 to 5 kayak runs from the bridge below Canyon Creek Campground down to the mouth.

■ EAST FORK LEWIS RIVER

Tributary of: Lewis River
Outstandingly Remarkable Values: Fish, recreation
Threats: Shoreline development
Segments & Classification
  Wild: 4 miles (source to Poison Gulch)
  Scenic: 18 miles (Poison Gulch to Lucia)

Special Values: This is probably the most heavily used recreational river in or near the Gifford Pinchot National Forest. It has outstanding rafting opportunities and is often frequented by fishermen in drift boats. It has produced some of the largest steelhead caught in Washington and is also a good salmon river.

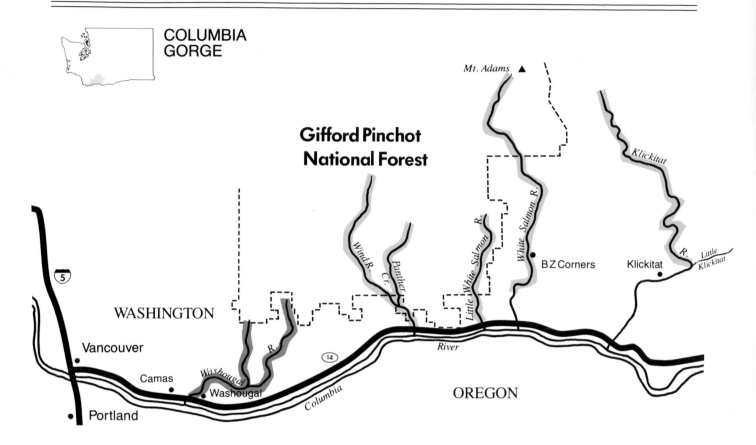

■ WASHOUGAL RIVER

Tributary of: Columbia River
Outstandingly Remarkable Values: Fish, scenery, recreation
Threats: Shoreline development
Segments & Classification
  State Scenic River: The Washougal River has been studied
  and recommended for designation as a state scenic river.
Special Values: The Washougal has fine runs of salmon and steelhead; beautiful Salmon Falls and Dougan Falls; and from Dougan Falls to Salmon Falls a kayak run. The river below Salmon Falls provides a moderately challenging raft and kayak run in the winter and early spring.

■ WIND RIVER

Tributary of: Columbia River
Outstandingly Remarkable Values: Fish, scenery
Threats: Hydroelectric projects, road building
Segments & Classification
  Wild: 3 miles (source to Oldman Creek)
  Scenic: 23 miles (Oldman Creek to Little Wind River)
  Scenic: 13 miles (source of Panther Creek to mouth)
Special Values: The Wind River is an outstanding anadromous fish stream, which Washington State manages for its wild steelhead run. Panther Creek is host to an important part of the anadromous runs on the Wind River. The portion of the river below Stabler (the lower 10 miles) rushes through a spectacular deep basalt gorge. This section also provides one of the finest kayak runs in the state.

■ LITTLE WHITE SALMON RIVER

Tributary of: Columbia River
Outstandingly Remarkable Values: Recreation, scenery, history
Threats: Hydropower
Segments & Classification
  Scenic: 14 miles (source to mouth, Drano Lake)
Special Values: The Little White Salmon River flows through a beautiful gorge and provides for some of the finest bank fishing and camping in the Gifford Pinchot National Forest. Its water powered the historic Broughton Flume, the last operating logging flume in the country.

■ WHITE SALMON RIVER

Tributary of: Columbia River
Outstandingly Remarkable Values: Scenery, recreation
Threats: Hydropower proposals
Segments & Classification
  Wild: 3 miles (source to Wilderness boundary)
  Scenic: 6 miles (Wilderness boundary to Ninefoot Creek)
  Wild: 5 miles (Ninefoot Creek to Green Canyon)
  Scenic: 15 miles (Green Canyon to Gilmer Creek)
  State Scenic River: The White Salmon has been studied and
  recommended for designation as a state scenic river.
Special Values: The river below Gilmer Creek is already designated as a Scenic river under the federal act. The White Salmon is fed by numerous springs gushing from the sides of its spectacular basalt canyon. The springs feed lush vegetation typical of Western Washington, though the White Salmon is just east of the divide. The river provides opportunities for kayaking and hiking as well as numerous secluded spots for camping and picnicking.

■ **KLICKITAT RIVER**
Tributary of: Columbia River
Outstandingly Remarkable Values: Fish, wildlife, scenery, recreation, geology
Threats: National Hydropower Inventory Dam Site
Segments & Classification
 Scenic: 4 miles (Dairy Creek—River Mile 50—to Deer Creek)
 Wild: 3 miles (Deer Creek to Trout Creek)
 Scenic: 24 miles (Trout Creek to Little Klickitat River)

Special Values: The Klickitat River is home to some of the finest runs of salmon and steelhead in the state. The canyon also provides outstanding wildlife habitat and is the site of the Department of Wildlife's Klickitat River Breaks Wildlife Management Area. The upper 18 miles of this section of the river provide one of the finest whitewater kayaking and rafting runs in the state, one of the highlights of which is the outstanding scenery. The canyon is set off by dramatic headwalls of columnar basalt towering hundreds of feet above the river.

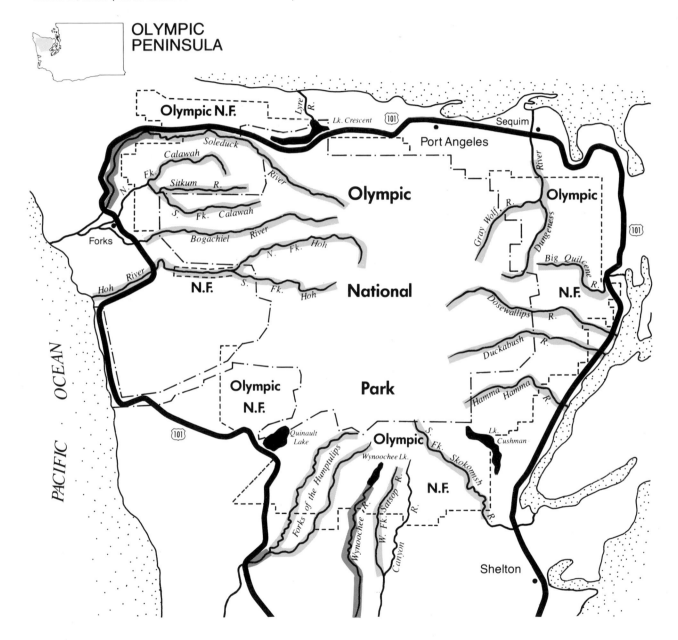

OLYMPIC PENINSULA

■ **SOUTH FORK SKOKOMISH**
Tributary of: Skokomish River
Outstandingly Remarkable Values: Fish, wildlife, ecology
Threats: Potential site of high dam at River Mile 9
Segments & Classification
 Wild: 4 miles (source to Rule Creek)

 Scenic: 21 miles (Rule Creek to national forest boundary)
Special Values: Coho and chinook salmon run up the river to above Church Creek and are very important to the Skokomish Indians, whose reservation is at the mouth of the river. The undisturbed upper 5 miles of the river constitute one of the few natural low-elevation riparian areas left on the Olympic Penin-

sula outside the National Park. Found here are old-growth forest, spotted owls, martens, and bald eagles.

■ HAMMA HAMMA RIVER

Tributary of: Hood Canal
Outstandingly Remarkable Values: Fish, scenery, recreation
Threats: Hydroelectric dams
Segments & Classification
  Wild: 3 miles (source to bridge on Forest Road 25)
  Scenic: 15 miles (bridge on Forest Road 25 to mouth)
Special Values: The lowest two miles of the Hamma Hamma River are particularly prolific producers of salmon. The river valley is heavily used for hiking, camping, picnicking, and other forms of dispersed recreation. There is a fine advanced kayak run from the bridge near Hamma Hamma Campground to just above the falls near mile 2. There are beautiful views of the river and the surrounding mountains from many points within the river corridor.

■ DUCKABUSH RIVER

Tributary of: Hood Canal
Outstandingly Remarkable Values: Scenery, fish, geology
Threats: Water-supply dam
Segments & Classification
  Wild: 17 miles (source to Little Hump)
  Scenic: 7 miles (Little Hump to mouth)
  State Scenic River: The Duckabush has been studied and
  recommended for designation as a state scenic river.
Special Values: The Duckabush River, with its spectacular scenery, fine salmon runs, numerous gorges, and extensive cliffs, is one of the outstanding rivers on the Olympic Peninsula. The Duckabush also features a kayak run from the end of the road to the mouth.

■ DOSEWALLIPS RIVER

Tributary of: Hood Canal
Outstandingly Remarkable Values: Fish, wildlife, scenery
Threats: Elkhorn hydroelectric project
Segments & Classification
  Wild: 14 miles (source to road end at Dosewallips Camp)
  Scenic: 14 miles (road end to mouth)
Special Values: Chinook, chum, coho, and pink salmon, and steelhead run strongly in the Dosewallips. The river valley provides critical winter range for many of the animals of the peninsula, particularly deer and elk. The river has spectacular scenery, including gorges, waterfalls, deep pools, and meadows at the foot of towering mountains.

■ BIG QUILCENE RIVER

Tributary of: Hood Canal
Outstandingly Remarkable Values: Wildlife, scenery, history
Threats: No current threats
Segments & Classification
  Wild: 4 miles (source to Wilderness boundary)
  Scenic: 12 miles (Wilderness boundary to Penny Creek)
Special Values: The Big Quilcene River runs from high meadows, cascades through old-growth forests and offers vistas of Olympic peaks. The substantial areas of undisturbed forest provide important habitat for spotted owls, martin, pileated woodpeckers, and winter big game range. The Big Quilcene trail is the historic northern access to Iron Mountain, Buckhorn Mountain, and the "Tubal Cain" mine.

■ DUNGENESS AND GRAY WOLF

Tributary of: Strait of Juan de Fuca
Outstandingly Remarkable Values: Fish, scenery
Threats: Hydroelectric projects
Segments & Classification
  Wild: 16 miles (source of Gray Wolf to bridge at River Mile 1)
  Wild: 4 miles (source of Dungeness to Forest Road
  2955 bridge)
  Scenic: 2 miles (Forest Road 2955 bridge to Silver Creek)
  Wild: 3.5 miles (Silver Creek to Gold Creek Bridge)
  Scenic: 1 mile (Gold Creek Bridge to East Crossing)
  Wild: 1.5 miles (East Crossing to the Forks)
  Scenic: 7 miles (Dungeness from the Forks to Fish Hatchery
  and Gray Wolf below bridge at River Mile 1)
Special Values: The Dungeness and Gray Wolf feature a unique pink salmon run, which is early enough in summer to avoid the lowest river flows. Both rivers have wonderful wilderness kayak runs, moderately difficult on the Dungeness and difficult on the Gray Wolf. The rivers also afford views of mountains, snowfields, cascading water, and narrow canyons.

■ LYRE RIVER

Tributary of: Strait of Juan de Fuca
Outstandingly Remarkable Values: Scenery, fish
Threats: Hydroelectric project
Segments & Classification
  Scenic: 5 miles (source—Lake Crescent—to mouth)
Special Values: The Lyre River follows a short but beautiful course from Lake Crescent to salt water, with beautiful deep pools and a wonderful falls. It is home to large numbers of chum salmon and significant numbers of chinook, coho, and pinks.

■ SOLEDUCK RIVER

Tributary of: Quillayute River
Outstandingly Remarkable Values: Fish, geology, recreation
Threats: Shoreline development
Segments & Classification
  Wild: 7 miles (source to end of Soleduck road)
  Scenic: 32 miles (end of road to Beaver Creek)
Special Values: The Soleduck River has some of the finest runs of salmon and steelhead in the state. It is a favorite with fishermen and one of the most challenging rivers run by fishermen in drift boats. It offers over 30 miles of good whitewater rafting and kayaking, and fascinating hot springs near its headwaters in Olympic National Park.

■ FORKS OF THE CALAWAH

Tributary of: Bogachiel River
Outstandingly Remarkable Values: Fish, recreation
Threats: Logging
Segments & Classification
  Wild: 15 miles (source of South Fork Calawah River to
  confluence with Sitkum River)
  Scenic: 6 miles (South Fork Calawah River from Sitkum
  River to confluence with North Fork Calawah River)
  Scenic: 13 miles (Sitkum River)
  Scenic: 21 miles (North Fork Calawah River)
Special Values: The forks of the Calawah provide spawning grounds for major runs of fall chinook and lesser runs of spring and summer chinook. Excellent runs of coho also spawn here, as well as small numbers of an unusual run of river-race sockeye.

Good kayak runs exist on all three major forks, particularly the Sitkum, which has excellent scenery and whitewater.

■ BOGACHIEL RIVER
Tributary of: Quillayute River
Outstandingly Remarkable Values: Fish, wildlife, scenery
Threats: No current threats
Segments & Classification
 Wild: 25 miles (source to Kahkwa Creek)
 Scenic: 6 miles (Kahkwa Creek to Bear Creek)
Special Values: The Bogachiel is one of the most productive anadromous fish streams on the Olympic Peninsula, hosting spring and fall chinook, coho, chum, and pink salmon as well as sea-run cutthroat trout. The upper river in the Olympic National Park is surrounded by old-growth rain forest and originates in snowfields in rugged mountains. The river corridor provides habitat for elk, deer, bear, and bald eagles.

■ HOH RIVER
Tributary of: Pacific Ocean
Outstandingly Remarkable Values: Scenery, fish, recreation, history
Threats: Hydroelectric dam
Segments & Classification
 Wild: 20 miles (source of North Fork Hoh River to National Park Ranger Station)
 Scenic: 6 miles (North Fork Hoh River from Ranger Station to National Park boundary)
 Recreation: 27 miles (North Fork Hoh River from Park boundary to mouth)
 Wild: 16 miles (source of South Fork Hoh River to end of road)
 Scenic: 2 miles (South Fork Hoh River from end of road to mouth)
Special Values: The Hoh originates with glaciers in the Olympic Mountains and flows through a highly diverse landscape including rare temperate rain forest. It is an important winter steelhead resource and sustains considerable canoeing and rafting as well as recreational fishing. The river is bordered by several historic ranches, including the Huelsdonk Place, home of John Huelsdonk, early pioneer, renowned as the "Iron Man of the Hoh."

■ FORKS OF THE HUMPTULIPS
Tributary of: Humptulips River
Outstandingly Remarkable Values: Scenery, fish, recreation
Threats: Logging
Segments & Classification
 Scenic: 30 miles (source of East Fork Hoh River to mouth)
 Scenic: 42 miles (source of West Fork Hoh River to mouth)
 State Scenic River: The Forks of the Humptulips and its main stem down to U.S. 101 have been studied and recommended for designation as a state scenic river.
Special Values: The Humptulips River has good runs of three different species of salmon, plus steelhead and sea-run cutthroat trout. There are several spectacular basalt gorges on the East Fork and a wide variety of recreational opportunities: good bank and boat fishing, easy canoeing on the West Fork and advanced whitewater kayaking and rafting on the East Fork.

■ WYNOOCHEE RIVER
Tributary of: Chehalis River
Outstandingly Remarkable Values: Fish, wildlife, geology
Threats: No current threats
Segments & Classification
 State Scenic River: The Wynoochee below the dam at river mile 50 has been studied and recommended for designation as a state scenic river.
Special Values: The Wynoochee River flows through a spectacular gorge that offers a challenging kayak run below the dam. There are good runs of salmon and steelhead on the river, making it popular with drift fishermen. Wildlife species include elk, deer, bear, and bald eagles.

■ WEST FORK SATSOP RIVER
Tributary of: Satsop River
Outstandingly Remarkable Values: Fish, scenery, recreation
Threats: No current threats
Segments & Classification
 Scenic: 17 miles (source to Canyon River)
Special Values: The lower half of the candidate segment provides good spawning and rearing habitat for coho, chinook, and chum salmon. It also flows through a beautiful gorge and provides an outstanding whitewater trip for kayakers. The river also provides important winter habitat for elk and deer.

Humptulips River Canyon, Olympic National Forest

The White Bluffs in afternoon light, Hanford Reach of the Columbia River

Questions About River Designation

Q: If dams are banned from all of these rivers, where will we get more power in the future?

In 1988 the Northwest Power Planning Council designated more than 12,000 miles of Washington rivers and streams as protected areas in which hydroelectric projects should not be built because of their importance to valuable fish and wildlife resources. Nearly all of the 2,200 miles of rivers and streams proposed for federal and state designation—amounting to less than 8 percent of the state total—are already protected under this program. Conservation of electric power through insulating homes, factories and offices and using more efficient appliances promises to be a much cheaper and larger source of additional energy in the future than hydroelectric power. The Power Planning Council has identified 2,500 megawatts of available conservation of this type (2,500 megawatts is the power equivalent of lighting up Seattle two and a half times).

Q: Will designation mean that the government will take away private land along the river?

Section 6(b) of the Wild and Scenic Rivers Act specifically forbids the federal government from taking away private property along rivers where the government already owns more than 50 percent of the land. Such is the case with all but one of the rivers in Washington along which people live. The Washington State Scenic Program cannot take private land under any circumstances.

Q: Will the government attempt to control development on private lands?

If a proposed development is clearly incompatible with national Wild and Scenic designation, or where there is a clear need for public access, the federal government can require a landowner to sell a scenic or conservation easement, wherein the landowner gives up certain development rights in return for a payment, while retaining title to the land. The landowner can continue to use the land as he has up to that point, including renting it, selling it or leaving it to his heirs, and restricting public access. The landowner does not lose land when an easement is purchased.

Q: How does river designation affect timber and agricultural practices?

State scenic designation has no effect on timber harvesting or farming. National Wild and Scenic designation does not significantly restrict timber harvesting on public land and has no effect on timber harvest or farming on private property unless the federal government buys a scenic or conservation easement. In fact, the Wild and Scenic Rivers Act states that "agricultural and forestry practices should be similar in nature as they were before designation." The 1988 Oregon Wild and Scenic Rivers bill, which designated more than 1,430 miles of 40 rivers, had an impact of less than one-tenth of one percent on the timber harvest. In general, past logging and agricultural practices can continue provided these activities do not degrade the outstanding qualities for which the river was designated.

Q: Wouldn't local control of river shorelines be preferable to state or federal control?

Ironically, the best way to assure a reasonable measure of local control over a river is for it to be designated in either the state or national river programs. Without designation, decisions that vitally effect the river are made elsewhere:

■ Dams are licensed in Washington, D.C.;
■ Mining permits are issued by the Bureau of Land Management in Portland for federal lands, and by the Washington State Department of Natural Resources in Olympia for private lands.
■ Decisions on road building and timber harvesting on National Forest land are made by the Regional Forester in Portland.

In contrast, river designation stops dams and provides a formal mechanism for implementing local participation in decisions on other types of development. The main feature of this process is the creation of a management plan for each river through public meetings in the affected watersheds.

Q: How does Wild and Scenic designation affect property values?

Property values and the local business climate either remain the same or improve slightly as a result of the distinction of being on a specially recognized river. For example, on the Delaware River (between New York and Pennsylvania) land values in the river corridor have doubled since designation in 1978, while nearby land outside the corridor has not increased in value. Property and business in Gold Beach and Grants Pass, Oregon have also benefitted greatly from having the National "Wild and Scenic" Rogue River nearby.

Q: Will designation increase recreational use and will there be more trespassing on private land?

Forest Service and BLM statistics show that river use usually increases only slightly or not at all directly as a result of designation. Trespassing should not increase; the managing agency will provide maps and signs to direct recreational use to publicly owned access sites. Recreational use of private lands is not allowed unless special arrangements are made with the landowner. Private landowners are entitled to post their property with "No Trespassing" signs.

Q: How does designation affect water rights?

State designation has no affect on water rights. Section 13(b) of the Wild and Scenic Rivers Act states that designation has no effect on existing water rights, but provides for the restriction of future water rights if necessary to maintain sufficient water for fish, wildlife, recreation, and scenic integrity.

Q: How does designation affect hunting and fishing along the river?

Neither state nor federal designation has any affect whatsoever on hunting or fishing.

Appendix to Part Three: Management Classification

The Forest Service handbook sets forth the following standards for management of the different river classifications:

1. Standards for Wild Rivers

a. *Timber Production:* Cutting of trees will not be permitted except when needed in association with a primitive recreation experience (such as clearing for trails and protection of users) or to protect the environment (such as control of fire). Timber outside the boundary but within the visual corridors, will be managed and harvested in a manner to provide special emphasis to visual quality.

b. *Water Supply:* All water supply dams and major diversions are prohibited.

c. *Hydroelectric Power:* No development of hydroelectric power facilities would be permitted.

d. *Flood Control:* No flood control dams, levees, or other works are allowed in the channel or river corridor. The natural appearance and essentially primitive character of the river area must be maintained.

e. *Mining:* New mining claims and mineral leases are prohibited within ¼ mile of the river. Valid claims would not be abrogated. Subject to regulations (36 CFR 228) that the Secretaries of Agriculture and Interior may prescribe to protect the rivers included in the National System, other existing mining activity would be allowed to continue. Existing mineral activity must be conducted in a manner that minimizes surface disturbance, sedi-

mentation, and visual impairment. Reasonable access will be permitted.

f. *Road Construction:* No roads or other provisions for overland motorized travel would be permitted within a narrow incised river valley or, if the river valley is broad, within ¼ mile of the river bank. A few inconspicuous roads leading to the boundary of the river area at the time of study will not disqualify wild river classification. Also, unobtrusive trail bridges could be allowed.

g. *Agriculture:* Agricultural use is restricted to a limited amount of domestic livestock grazing and hay production to the extent currently practiced. Row crops are prohibited.

h. *Recreation Development:* Major public-use areas, such as large campgrounds, interpretive centers, or administrative headquarters are located outside the wild river area. Simple comfort and convenience facilities, such as fireplaces or shelters may be provided as necessary within the river area. These should harmonize with the surroundings.

i. *Structure:* A few minor existing structures could be allowed assuming such structures are not incompatible with the essentially primitive and natural values of the viewshed. New structures would not be allowed except in rare instances to achieve management objectives (i.e. structures and activities associated with fisheries enhancement programs could be allowed).

j. *Utilities:* New transmission lines, gas lines, water lines, etc. are discouraged. Where no reasonable alternative exists, additional or new facilities should be restricted to existing rights-of-way. Where new rights-of-way are indicated, the scenic, recreational, and fish and wildlife values must be evaluated in the selection of the site.

k. *Motorized travel:* Motorized travel on land or water could be permitted, but is generally not compatible with this classification.

2. Standards for Scenic Rivers

a. *Timber Production:* A wide range of silvicultural practices could be allowed provided that such practices are carried on in such a way that there is no substantial adverse effect on the river and its immediate environment. The river area should be maintained in its near-natural environment. Timber outside the boundary but within the visual scene area should be managed and harvested in a manner which provides special emphasis on visual quality.

b. *Water Supply:* All water supply dams and major diversions are prohibited.

c. *Hydroelectric Power:* No development of hydroelectric power facilities would be allowed.

d. *Flood Control:* Flood control dams and levees would be prohibited.

e. *Mining:* Subject to regulations at 36 CFR 228 that the Secretaries of Agriculture and the Interior may prescribe to protect the values of rivers included in the National System, new mining claims and mineral leases could be allowed and existing operations allowed to continue. However, mineral activity must be conducted in a manner that minimizes surface disturbance, sedimentation and pollution, and visual impairment.

f. *Road Construction:* Roads may occasionally bridge the river area and short stretches of conspicuous or longer stretches of inconspicuous and well-screened roads or screened railroads could be allowed. Consideration will be given to the type of use for which roads are constructed and the type of use that will occur in the river area.

g. *Agriculture:* A wider range of agricultural uses is permitted to the extent currently practiced. Row crops are not considered as an intrusion of the "largely primitive" nature of scenic corridors as long as there is not a substantial adverse effect on the natural-like appearance of the river area.

h. *Recreation Development:* Larger scale public-use facilities, such as moderate size campgrounds, public information centers, and administrative headquarters are allowed if such structures are screened from the river. Modest and unobtrusive marinas also can be allowed.

i. *Structures:* Any concentrations of habitations are limited to relatively short reaches of the river corridor. New structures that would have a direct and adverse effect on river values would not be allowed.

j. *Utilities:* This is the same as for wild river classifications.

k. *Motorized Travel:* Motorized travel on land or water may be permitted, prohibited or restricted to protect the river values.

3. Standards for Recreational Rivers

a. *Timber Production:* Timber harvesting would be allowed under standard restrictions to protect the immediate river environment, water quality, scenic, fish and wildlife, and other values.

b. *Water Supply:* Existing low dams, diversion works, rip rap and other minor structures are allowed provided the waterway remains generally natural in appearance. New structures are prohibited.

c. *Hydroelectric Power:* No development of hydroelectric power facilities is allowed.

d. *Flood Control:* Existing flood control works may be maintained. New structures are prohibited.

e. *Mining:* Subject to regulations (36 CFR 228) that the Secretaries of Agriculture and the Interior may prescribe to protect values of rivers included in the National System, new mining claims and mineral leases are allowed and existing operations are allowed to continue. Mineral activity must be conducted in a manner that minimizes surface disturbance, sedimentation and pollution, and visual impairment.

f. *Road Construction:* Paralleling roads or railroads could be constructed in one or both river banks. There can be several bridge crossings and numerous river access points.

g. *Agriculture:* Lands may be managed for a full range of agricultural uses, to the extent currently practiced.

h. *Recreation Development:* Campgrounds and picnic areas may be established in close proximity to the river. However, recreational classification does not require extensive recreation development.

i. *Structures:* Small communities as well as dispersed or cluster residential developments are allowed. New structures are allowed for both habitation and for intensive recreation use.

j. *Utilities:* This is the same as for wild and scenic river classifications.

k. *Motorized Travel:* Motorized travel on land or water may be permitted, prohibited or restricted. Controls will usually be similar to surrounding lands and waters.

INDEX

Keith Lazelle

AUTHOR TIM MCNULTY is a poet, writer, and conservationist whose work has taken him throughout the mountains and river canyons of the West. Since obtaining a degree in literature from the University of Massachusetts in 1971, Tim has authored several books of poetry and has published numerous articles on wildlife, wilderness, and forestry issues. With photographer Pat O'Hara, he has co-authored an award-winning series of books on National Parks, which includes *Mount Rainier National Park, Realm of the Sleeping Giant,* and *Olympic National Park, Where the Mountain Meets the Sea.* Tim lives with his wife Mary and their daughter along the Little Quilcene River on Washington's Olympic Peninsula.

Laura Lilly

PHOTOGRAPHER PAT O'HARA first developed an interest in nature photography while exploring the Yakima River corridor as a student at Central Washington University at Ellensburg. He received a Master of Forest Resources from the University of Washington in 1976. He has worked as a professional photographer since 1979, and his work has appeared in numerous publications including: *American Photographer, Audubon, Backpacker, Outside,* and *National Geographic.* Pat's color photography has been featured in ten large-format books including *Washington Wilderness, The Unfinished Work,* published in 1984 by The Mountaineers Books. Pat lives with his wife Tina and their daughter Trisha in the Olympic foothills south of Port Angeles, Washington.

DOUGLASS A. NORTH, author and Washington native, practices law in Seattle. A founder of the Northwest Rivers Council, he has been very active in protecting the rivers of the Northwest from development that would interfere with their free-flowing qualities and the recreation, fish, and wildlife dependent on them.

ARTIST JIM HAYS created the fourteen watercolor illustrations that appear as chapter opening accents for this book. He was born and raised in Washington and is deeply involved with the Northwest environment.